Sexually Transmitted Diseases

Other Books in the Current Controversies Series:

Sexually Transmitted Diseases

Bryan J. Grapes, *Book Editor*

Bonnie Szumski, *Editorial Director*
Scott Barbour, *Managing Editor*

CURRENT CONTROVERSIES

Cover photo: © Michael Newman / Photo Edit

Library of Congress Cataloging-in-Publication Data

Sexually transmitted diseases / Bryan J. Grapes, book editor
        p. cm. — (Current controversies)
    Includes bibliographical references and index.
    ISBN 0-7377-0686-4 (pbk. : alk. paper) — ISBN 0-7377-0687-2
(lib. bdg. : alk. paper)
    1. Sexually transmitted diseases. I. Grapes, Bryan J. II. Series.

RC200 .S4952   2001
616.95'1—dc21   2001-018751
                                                                              CIP

© 2001 by Greenhaven Press, Inc., PO Box 289009, San Diego, CA 92198-9009
Printed in the U.S.A.

Every effort has been made to trace the owners of copyrighted material.

Contents

Chapter 3: How Can Sexually Transmitted Diseases Be Prevented?

Chapter 4: Should Public Health Measures Be Used to Prevent the Spread of HIV?

Foreword

By definition, controversies are "discussions of questions in which opposing opinions clash" (Webster's Twentieth Century Dictionary Unabridged). Few would deny that controversies are a pervasive part of the human condition and exist on virtually every level of human enterprise. Controversies transpire between individuals and among groups, within nations and between nations. Controversies supply the grist necessary for progress by providing challenges and challengers to the status quo. They also create atmospheres where strife and warfare can flourish. A world without controversies would be a peaceful world; but it also would be, by and large, static and prosaic.

The Series' Purpose

The purpose of the Current Controversies series is to explore many of the social, political, and economic controversies dominating the national and international scenes today. Titles selected for inclusion in the series are highly focused and specific. For example, from the larger category of criminal justice, Current Controversies deals with specific topics such as police brutality, gun control, white collar crime, and others. The debates in Current Controversies also are presented in a useful, timeless fashion. Articles and book excerpts included in each title are selected if they contribute valuable, long-range ideas to the overall debate. And wherever possible, current information is enhanced with historical documents and other relevant materials. Thus, while individual titles are current in focus, every effort is made to ensure that they will not become quickly outdated. Books in the Current Controversies series will remain important resources for librarians, teachers, and students for many years.

In addition to keeping the titles focused and specific, great care is taken in the editorial format of each book in the series. Book introductions and chapter prefaces are offered to provide background material for readers. Chapters are organized around several key questions that are answered with diverse opinions representing all points on the political spectrum. Materials in each chapter include opinions in which authors clearly disagree as well as alternative opinions in which authors may agree on a broader issue but disagree on the possible solutions. In this way, the content of each volume in Current Controversies mirrors the mosaic of opinions encountered in society. Readers will quickly realize that there are many viable answers to these complex issues. By questioning each au-

9

thor's conclusions, students and casual readers can begin to develop the critical thinking skills so important to evaluating opinionated material.

Current Controversies is also ideal for controlled research. Each anthology in the series is composed of primary sources taken from a wide gamut of informational categories including periodicals, newspapers, books, United States and foreign government documents, and the publications of private and public organizations. Readers will find factual support for reports, debates, and research papers covering all areas of important issues. In addition, an annotated table of contents, an index, a book and periodical bibliography, and a list of organizations to contact are included in each book to expedite further research.

Perhaps more than ever before in history, people are confronted with diverse and contradictory information. During the Persian Gulf War, for example, the public was not only treated to minute-to-minute coverage of the war, it was also inundated with critiques of the coverage and countless analyses of the factors motivating U.S. involvement. Being able to sort through the plethora of opinions accompanying today's major issues, and to draw one's own conclusions, can be a complicated and frustrating struggle. It is the editors' hope that Current Controversies will help readers with this struggle.

Greenhaven Press anthologies primarily consist of previously published material taken from a variety of sources, including periodicals, books, scholarly journals, newspapers, government documents, and position papers from private and public organizations. These original sources are often edited for length and to ensure their accessibility for a young adult audience. The anthology editors also change the original titles of these works in order to clearly present the main thesis of each viewpoint and to explicitly indicate the opinion presented in the viewpoint. These alterations are made in consideration of both the reading and comprehension levels of a young adult audience. Every effort is made to ensure that Greenhaven Press accurately reflects the original intent of the authors included in this anthology.

"While most people agree that healthy and responsible sexual behaviors should be promoted . . . profound disagreements exist as to what constitutes responsible behaviors."

Introduction

Sexually transmitted diseases (STDs), also called venereal diseases, are caused by germs that travel from person to person through sexual contact. Common STDs include syphilis, chlamydia, genital herpes, gonorrhea, and AIDS. Because the germs that cause STDs die quickly outside the human body, these sicknesses are not spread through coughing, sneezing, or contact with infected objects such as toilet seats or eating utensils. Most STDs, however, can be transmitted from an infected pregnant woman to her baby, often causing serious and life-threatening complications for the infant. Some viral diseases, including AIDS and hepatitis B, are spread through direct exposure to infected blood and can be transmitted through sexual contact or through nonsexual means such as the sharing of needles for drug use.

Sexually transmitted diseases have become a serious health problem in the United States. The Institute of Medicine, an arm of the National Academy of Sciences, asserts that STDs are prevalent and constitute a "hidden epidemic" because of the reluctance of Americans to "address sexual health issues in an open way." With twelve million new cases a year, America has one of the highest rates of STD infection in the industrialized world. STDs (including AIDS) cost the United States an estimated $17 billion in health care costs each year.

Chlamydia, a bacterial infection, is the most common sexually transmitted disease in the United States, affecting at least four million Americans annually. It is one of several STDs that can cause pelvic inflammatory disease—the inflammation of a woman's reproductive tract, which if left untreated can lead to infertility and death. The effects of other STDs vary. Genital herpes can create blistering and discomfort. The human papillomavirus (HPV) may cause cervical cancer. AIDS can fatally impair the body's immune system.

Young people are especially at risk for many sexually transmitted diseases. Teenagers account for three million cases of STDs annually. One out of every four sexually active teenagers acquires a new STD each year. One-quarter of new infections of HIV (the virus that causes AIDS) are found in people under twenty-two. Young women are at greater risk than older women for reproductive and health complications caused by STDs.

The medical options for the treatment and prevention of sexually transmitted diseases are somewhat limited. Some bacterial STDs, including chlamydia, syphilis, and gonorrhea, can be treated with antibiotics if detected early enough (although the evolution of new germs resistant to antibiotics is a growing problem). Antibiotics are useless against viral STDs, however. Public health measures have therefore focused primarily on preventing the spread of STDs. Because vaccinations for STDs are still in the research stage, efforts to prevent STDs have centered on reducing risky sexual activities. Yet while most people agree that healthy and responsible sexual behaviors should be promoted in the media, in clinics, and in sex education classes, profound disagreements exist as to what constitutes responsible behaviors.

For some people, responsible and disease-preventing behavior is synonymous with sexual restraint. They believe that everyone should be taught that abstaining from sex altogether or confining sex within a mutually monogamous relationship are the only 100 percent effective methods of keeping oneself free of all sexually transmitted diseases. Engaging in sex with multiple partners and relying on condoms to prevent STDs, in this view, is risky because condoms sometimes break, are not used properly, or are simply ineffective. Many advocates of abstinence criticize sex education programs in schools for including information on condoms and "safe sex," arguing that such a curriculum gives teenagers a false sense of security about sex and fails to discourage sexual activity. "To present 'protected' sex as an alternative to abstinence is inadequate," argues Joe S. McIlhaney, a gynecologist and founder of the Medical Institute for Sexual Health. "The best that 'safer sex' approaches can offer is some risk reduction. Abstinence, on the other hand, offers risk elimination. When the risks of pregnancy and disease are so great, even with contraception, how can we advocate anything less?"

Most people agree that abstinence is the most effective way of preventing sexually transmitted diseases and that people should be made aware that certain activities—including sex at an early age and sex with multiple partners or prostitutes—greatly increase the risks of contracting STDs. But many sex education authorities, such as Debra W. Haffner of the Sexuality Information and Education Council of the U.S., contend that abstinence should not be the sole emphasis of STD prevention and sex education programs. Americans should acknowledge that many teenagers are engaging in sexual activity, Haffner and others maintain. Studies have found that the average age of first intercourse in the United States is sixteen and that two-thirds of America's high school seniors are sexually experienced prior to graduation. Haffner argues that, given the reality that many teenagers reject the option of abstinence, young people should be given comprehensive sexuality information "about their bodies, gender roles, sexual abuse, pregnancy, and STD prevention," including the proper use of condoms to prevent diseases. She asserts that "fear-based, abstinence-only programs" that "discuss contraception only in negative terms" threaten to reverse "the significant strides American youth have made during the last two decades to delay sexual activity or else protect themselves."

Introduction

The pros and cons of abstinence-only sex education are just some of the arguments that surround STDs. The dangers posed by sexually transmitted diseases, and how those diseases can be prevented, are the subjects of *Sexually Transmitted Diseases: Current Controversies*. In this book, the authors debate whether sexually transmitted diseases are a serious problem, what populations are at the greatest risk of contracting those diseases, how STDs can be prevented, and the role of public health measures in reducing the spread of HIV.

Chapter 1

Are Sexually Transmitted Diseases a Serious Problem?

Chapter Preface

According to the Centers for Disease Control and Prevention, nearly half of all high school students have engaged in sexual intercourse. Not surprisingly, sexually transmitted diseases are a growing problem among teenagers—three million teens are infected with an STD each year. Although AIDS often gets the most attention, other STDs are considerably more common among teenagers, in particular gonorrhea. Gonorrhea, which is marked by a pus-like discharge from the cervix or penis, can be treated with penicillin or other antibiotics. If left untreated, the infection can spread into the testicles, causing sterility, or into the uterus and Fallopian tubes, leading to pelvic inflammatory disease. Gonorrhea can also infect the pharynx, or the upper part of the throat.

In its "Trends in STDs in the United States, 2000" the CDC reports that the incidence of gonorrhea among women is greatest between the ages of 15 and 19. In 1999, approximately 198 out of every 100,000 white females in that age group were infected. For African American women of that age, the ratio was 3,691 per 100,000. The rates for white males and African American males in that age group were approximately 116 and 3,582 per 100,000, respectively. Although those rates are considerably lower than in the mid-1980s, they are a 13 percent increase from 1997.

One reason why gonorrhea remains one of the most common STDs among teenagers is a lack of awareness about the disease. Although 58 percent of teenagers in 1999 used condoms during intercourse, compared to 46 percent in 1991, teens are not wholly aware of how the disease can be transmitted. In an article in *USA Today*, Karen S. Peterson writes that many teenagers are unaware of the health risks of oral sex, such as the possibility of contracting gonorrhea of the pharynx.

The extent of sexually transmitted diseases, whether among adolescents or adults, remains a matter of debate. In the following chapter, the authors explore whether STDs are a serious problem or if the dangers are overstated.

The Incidence of Sexually Transmitted Diseases Is Increasing

by Susan Burner Bankowski and Brandon Bankowski

About the author: *Susan Burner Bankowski is associate director of Campaign for Our Children, a national nonprofit organization that encourages healthy sexual behavior among youth. Brandon Bankowski is a resident physician in the department of obstetrics and gynecology at Johns Hopkins Hospital in Baltimore, Maryland.*

The spread of sexually transmitted diseases has reached staggering proportions on a global scale, yet hardly anyone wants to talk about them.

With the pervasive use of sex as a marketing tool and the romanticizing of "worry-free sex" in magazines, on television, and in the movies, it is easy to see why sexual promiscuity has increased greatly over the past 50 years. But the tragedy that generally goes unpublicized is the accompanying rampant spread of sexually transmitted diseases (STDs).

These diseases affect millions of people worldwide. But because they have historically carried a stigma and have been associated with shame, STDs have been largely absent from public discussion. With the advent of AIDS (acquired immune deficiency syndrome) in the 1980s, public awareness of STDs has increased, but there is still far too little known about them. For the most part, STDs are a silent epidemic.

It now appears that, on a global level, at least 1 in 4 persons will contract an STD at some point in his or her life. More than 12 million Americans, including 3 million teenagers, are infected with an STD each year. In the United States alone, as many as 56 million adults and adolescents may already have a lifetime incurable viral STD other than the human immunodeficiency virus (HIV), which leads to AIDS. Moreover, when it comes to contracting curable STDs, this nation has the highest incidence in the developed world.

Many STDs occur without symptoms, are more severe in women, and often go undetected until permanent damage has occurred. If left untreated, they can lead to long-term complications, including severe pain, infertility, birth defects, various cancers and other diseases, and even death. Young adults are at greatest risk of acquiring STDs, for reasons that include having many sexual partners, partners who are more likely to have an infection, and lower use of contraceptives. As well, the public and private costs of STDs are immense. Conservative estimates of total costs are around $10 billion in the United States, rising to $17 billion if HIV infections are included.

Fortunately, STDs are preventable. The problem is that most people don't know much about them, and this lack of knowledge leads to so many infections that could have been prevented.

Two Common Infections

A young married woman goes to the doctor for a routine checkup. It has been over a year since her last exam. She and her husband have been trying to conceive a child for the past few months but without success. She's not worried, though.

"Everything OK?" she asks assumingly. No, everything is not all right. The doctor informs the woman that she has contracted a sexually transmitted disease called chlamydia.

"That's not possible," she says. "I'm married and my husband doesn't have it. Besides, wouldn't I be able to feel it or see it?" The doctor proceeds

> *"More than 12 million Americans, including 3 million teenagers, are infected with an STD each year."*

to explain that one of them may have contracted the infection recently or could have harbored it for a long time without any symptoms. Either way, she has been infected with a bacterial species that has caused her to have a condition known as PID (pelvic inflammatory disease), which may render her unable to bear children.

Chlamydia and gonorrhea are the most common of all sexually transmitted diseases, with an estimated 4 million new cases of chlamydia and 1 million new cases of gonorrhea in the United States each year. Actually, chlamydia is the most common communicable disease in all developed countries, and it is the fastest spreading STD in the United States.

Chlamydia and gonorrhea often occur simultaneously and are similar in many ways. Both are bacterial infections, the causative agents being Chlamydia trachomatis and Neisseria gonorrhoeae, respectively. They are spread by contact with infected body fluids, such as semen and vaginal secretions, or with mucous membranes, such as those lining the mouth, vagina, and rectum. Between 25 and 40 percent of women who have gonorrhea also have chlamydia.

Gonorrhea, also referred to as "the clap" or "the drip," leads to a puslike discharge from the penis or cervix. It also causes pain in the lower abdomen and a painful, burning sensation when urinating. But among women, 30–80 percent of infections are asymptomatic, while for men that figure is below 5 percent. Chlamydia is less obvious and trickier to detect: As many as 85 percent of infected women and about 40 percent of infected men have no symptoms.

In infected women, when symptoms such as lower belly pain do occur, it is often because the bacteria have permanently scarred the woman's reproductive system. This damage may lead to infertility or a dangerous ectopic pregnancy—that is, the fetus may start growing outside the uterus. Alternatively, even if the pregnancy is carried to term, both diseases can be transmitted to the baby during vaginal delivery, causing eye infections and chronic pneumonia in newborns. It is therefore very important for a pregnant woman to obtain prenatal testing and care. Both infections can be cured with one dose of antibiotics taken orally.

> *"Chlamydia and gonorrhea are the most common of all sexually transmitted diseases, with an estimated 4 million new cases of chlamydia . . . each year."*

More than a Rash

A young man notices that the palms of his hands have acquired a rash that persists for several days, no matter what creams or lotions he applies. A week or two later, at the insistence of his girlfriend, he decides to go to the doctor. After running some blood tests, the physician informs him that the rash is a symptom of syphilis that has spread throughout his body. Explaining the risks involved with the disease, the doctor recommends that he and his girlfriend get treated immediately. The young man is surprised, saying that he never noticed any symptoms "down there." But he is also fearful, so he takes the doctor's advice and accepts treatment.

There are around 120,000 new cases of syphilis in the United States each year. The disease, which is caused by the bacterial species Treponema pallidum, affects the body in stages. The first stage is characterized by a painless, hard, red sore called a chancre, which appears at the site where the person is first infected—often the mouth, penis, or vagina. The sore may be as small as a pimple or as large as a dime. After several weeks, the chancre "resolves" (disappears), but that doesn't mean that the disease is gone. Direct contact with one of these lesions will transmit the bacteria to another person. The infectious agent may also be transmitted to a fetus through the placenta. At this stage, syphilis may be easily treated with an antibiotic such as penicillin.

If untreated, the patient generally develops secondary or "disseminated" syphilis, roughly six months after the initial sore has cleared up. This stage may be recognized by a flaking, nonitchy rash on the palms of the hands, the soles of the feet, or all over the body. Other symptoms may include fever, weight loss, and swollen lymph nodes. This stage may last several weeks to months, but it will also go away on its own.

If the infection is still not treated, tertiary syphilis may occur, which can permanently damage the brain, eyes, bones, or heart and may even lead to death. If caught in time, this stage requires weeks of hospitalization and treatment with drugs given intravenously. The damage is often irreversible.

Sore Spots

A pregnant woman traveling far from home suddenly goes into labor and is rushed to a hospital. The obstetrician, unfamiliar with her medical history, asks her a number of questions, including whether she's had any STD in the past. She says she once had herpes but doesn't have it now. Luckily, the doctor examines her cervix and vagina, for her cervix has a herpes sore of which she was unaware. The doctor then delivers the baby by cesarean section, to prevent the child from contacting the sore and getting a potentially brain-damaging infection.

In the United States alone, about 40 million people have been infected with the herpes simplex virus (HSV), and 300,000–500,000 new cases are reported each year. The virus, which has two common strains (HSV types I and II), causes painful sores around the mouth and on the genitals. Any touching of a herpes sore may transmit the virus to another person or another part of one's own body, including the eyes.

> *"There are around 120,000 new cases of syphilis in the United States each year."*

The sores generally last two to three weeks before going away on their own. But half the number of infected people get recurrent outbreaks of the painful sores for many years, potentially for the rest of their lives. Some studies have shown that herpes increases a woman's risk for cervical cancer. There is no cure for herpes, but expensive antiviral medicines may decrease the symptoms or shorten the duration of the outbreaks.

If a baby is delivered during an active outbreak of the disease, it can acquire a deadly brain infection known as meningitis. An outbreak may be hard to detect because the lesions are often inside the vagina or on the cervix. Babies should be delivered by cesarean section if the mother has active herpes.

Hepatitis B

The doctor who prescribed antibiotic treatment for the young woman with chlamydia follows up with a recommendation that she get a vaccine against hepatitis as well. "But why would I need that?" she protests. The doctor explains that people who have an STD are at greater risk for hepatitis B as well, because their sexual partners could very likely carry other infections and because any lesions will make transmission easier.

Hepatitis B is a dangerous virus that attacks the liver. About 200,000 people get "hep B" each year. It is contracted through oral, vaginal, or anal intercourse, sharing drug needles or other piercing equipment, or being exposed to infected blood. If a person gets the virus, it may take up to five months before causing a flulike syndrome, with nausea, vomiting, stomach pain, and headaches. As the disease progressively destroys the liver, the patient's skin may turn yellow (a condition called jaundice) and he may become very ill.

Often the infection resolves on its own in one or two months, but some people remain chronically infected—that is, the disease remains in their system. Most of the latter cases show no symptoms, but the virus can still be transmitted to other people. In about 4 percent of cases, the infection is fatal. Treatment of an active case of the disease may involve complicated, multidrug therapy.

> *"In the United States alone, about 40 million people have been infected with the herpes simplex virus."*

Hepatitis B is the only STD for which there is a vaccine: A series of three shots prevents a person from contracting the disease. If you think you may be at risk, or if your sexual partner has hepatitis, ask your doctor to test you for the virus.

HIV: An Insidious Agent

The bus is crowded with the usual group of morning passengers. A teenage boy, riding to high school, recognizes many of the faces. As his eyes scan the advertisements along the side of the bus, they stop at a new ad that reads, "48 teens were infected with HIV . . . today." He looks at the others riding to school with him and wonders which of his friends may already have been infected. There's no way he can tell just by looking at them.

The human immunodeficiency virus (HIV) is an insidious agent that gradually weakens and destroys a person's immune system. As a result, someone who has been infected with the virus for a long time readily succumbs to infections by other pathogens. These "opportunistic" infections lead to diseases that are collectively known as AIDS. Thus, while HIV itself does not kill the patient, the development of AIDS does.

Roughly a million people in the United States have HIV, and 45,000 more contract the virus each year via sexual contact, shared needles, contact with infected blood, and breast-feeding. Women are the fastest-growing segment of the infected population. Worldwide, 75 percent of HIV infections stem from sexual activity, 10 percent result from intravenous drug use, and 10 percent are vertically transmitted from infected mother to baby. Eighty percent of the sexually transmitted HIV occurs by heterosexual contact. Someone who has had other STDs is at increased risk of getting HIV.

People infected with HIV often show no symptoms for weeks or months. The first evidence of the disease may be a flulike illness that occurs when the patient undergoes "sero-conversion"—that is, when the virus can be detected in the blood by a lab test. It may take six months from the time of infection before the tests give a positive result. This means that someone whose test result is negative may still have HIV and be able to transmit the infection to someone else.

HIV is a slow-acting but complicated virus. Because it frequently mutates inside the patient's body, it is quite difficult to treat. As the infection progresses, the amount of virus in the bloodstream increases, while the number of "CD4" immune cells (which are attacked by the virus) decreases. At present, there is no cure for the infection, but the patient may need to take up to 18 pills a day to fight the infection and prolong his life. These medications (called antiretrovirals) are not only expensive but may have strong side effects that make the person feel very ill.

An HIV-infected woman can transmit the virus to her child during pregnancy or when breast-feeding. Certain drug therapies, called ZDV or AZT, can greatly reduce the risk of transmission during pregnancy. It is also recommended that HIV-positive women deliver via cesarean section and when their "viral load" (concentration of virus in the blood) is low, but both these techniques are still being investigated. In addition, an HIV-positive woman should avoid breast-feeding, unless, as in some developing countries that have high infant mortality rates, the deprivation of breast milk with its natural immunities would be life threatening to the child.

> *"Roughly a million people in the United States have HIV, and 45,000 more contract the virus each year via sexual contact."*

In addition to the aforementioned infections, there are many other STDs that are harrowing if not just as threatening. They include trichomoniasis (a parasitic infection), pubic lice, scabies, chancroid, and human papillomavirus, the last of which often causes genital warts and may further cause penile and cervical cancers.

Preventing STDs

We need to remind ourselves that STDs are preventable. Effective prevention should include both individual education and population-based approaches. Whether the education consists of a one-on-one dialogue, classroom-style lecturing, or mass-media dissemination, it enables individuals to make informed decisions and protect themselves from these diseases by changing risky behaviors. Good STD-prevention education needs to include several vital components:

• Knowledge of the disease, conveying the mode of transmission, the symptoms, and the treatment. It is important to note that disappearance of the symptoms does not mean that the disease has been cured and cannot be transmitted to others. Also, many STDs are transmitted in ways other than sexual intercourse.

• Abstinence-based education, which emphasizes that the safest way to avoid contracting an STD is not to engage in sexual activity outside of a mutually faithful relationship. Remember, it is impossible to tell if a person is disease free by simply looking at him or her, and a potential partner may be symptom free but still harbor an infection.

• The understanding that while certain STDs are curable, others are not. The problem is complicated by the emergence of strains of pathogenic microbes that are resistant to antibiotics.

• The knowledge that it is safest for both partners to be tested for all STDs before having sex, regardless of whether they plan on using "barrier methods" such as condoms or dental dams.

• Stressing the importance of maintaining a monogamous relationship once the partners have been tested.

• Education about the dangers of intravenous drug use and needle sharing.

In addition to education and counseling, critical components of population-based prevention and control include: (1) screening high-risk populations for prevalent STDs; (2) treating individuals with diagnosed and probable infections; and (3) reporting STD cases to the Health Department.

These approaches are extremely important for many reasons. Foremost is the health and well-being of the population. Better knowledge about STDs will reduce their transmission and result in fewer people becoming infected. In addition, screening and knowledge about risks and symptoms will reduce the degree of long-term damage to infected individuals. On a policy level, prevention and early treatment are cost effective. It is far less expensive to prevent a disease than to treat it, and the early

> *"We need to remind ourselves that STDs are preventable."*

stages of infection are not as costly to treat as the more advanced stages.

In conclusion, sexually transmitted diseases silently impair the lives and futures of millions of people each year worldwide. Although all STDs are preventable and many are curable, they impose enormous social, physical, and financial burdens on individuals and on society as a whole. Advocacy and funding for education, screening, treatment, reporting, and behavior modification must be continued in order to stop this epidemic and reduce the rates of sexually transmitted infections.

The Rate of Herpes Infection Is Increasing

by Betsy Carpenter

About the author: *Betsy Carpenter is a contributing editor for* U.S. News & World Report.

Fifteen years ago, genital herpes had the sexually permissive in a panic. One in 10 adults was thought to be stricken with this ancient, incurable venereal disease and its accompanying blisters and sores. Suddenly, "free" sex seemed very costly; here was a consequence of a one-night stand that the pill couldn't avert and penicillin couldn't remedy. Then herpes seemed to vanish, eclipsed in the public's mind by the swift, deadly rise of AIDS.

But the virus didn't go away: It surged to create an epidemic. According to a study published in the October 1997 edition of the *New England Journal of Medicine*, since the late 1970s, the proportion of Americans infected with the herpes simplex type 2 virus (HSV-2) has increased by almost one third. Today, 45 million people over the age of 12 carry it—about 1 in 5. Women generally are more susceptible to sexually transmitted diseases (STDs), so the numbers climb even higher for women. One in five white women is infected, versus one in seven white men. One in two black women has the virus, compared with one in three black men.

To Anna Wald, medical director of the Virology Research Clinic at the University of Washington in Seattle, "Herpes has become a major public health problem." In addition to causing sufferers periodic pain and discomfort, genital herpes is potentially devastating to newborns exposed during delivery. Herpes has also been shown to confound the lives of people with suppressed immune systems, such as burn victims and transplant patients. Recent studies show that people with herpes are more susceptible to a variety of STDs, including HIV—the virus that causes AIDS.

Several misconceptions about herpes are fueling the epidemic, according to public-health experts. Most Americans think the virus is uncommon, for instance, afflicting 1 percent or less of the population, says Peggy Clarke, former president of the American Social Health Association in Research Triangle Park in North Carolina. "People just don't know how likely they are to pick it up [from a prospective partner] unless they take precautions."

Many people also hold the mistaken belief that the herpes virus that infects the mouth is benign (herpes simplex type 1 or HSV-1) and that the one that infects the genitals is malevolent (HSV-2). There are differences between the two: HSV-1, which is far more prevalent, infecting about 7 in 10 people, often is acquired in childhood and usually infects the mouth; HSV-2 is typically acquired sexually and usually infects the genitals. But the two are clinically indistinguishable and can inhabit each other's territory. Oral-genital sex is an increasing source of infections, with perhaps 15 percent of genital sores really a manifestation of an HSV-1 infection. "People need to think of [lip] cold sores as infectious to newborns and sexual partners, too," says virologist Rhoda Ashley of the University of Washington in Seattle.

In addition, studies have shown that 2 out of 3 people with the virus don't know they are infected and potentially contagious. How can they miss clusters of itching, painful blisters? For many, a first outbreak is hard to ignore—like a bad case of the flu plus lesions. But others, especially individuals who already harbor HSV-1, often experience only a mild primary infection with HSV-2— with symptoms more like paper cuts or pimples than blisters. According to Ashley, the symptoms can be so variable that "even skilled practitioners can miss [herpes]." Some people also may be refusing to face facts. According to one study, 40 percent to 75 percent of the people with genital herpes who claim to have never experienced symptoms are able to identify them after a doctor delivers the news that they are infected.

No "Safe" Time

Many believe that people who carry herpes are infectious only during acute episodes, when blisters erupt. Yet infected people can shed virus particles from the genital area—and enough of them to infect a sexual partner—even when they are lesion free. Recent research with a new, sensitive test reveals that even when women with HSV-2 have no visible symptoms, they are shedding the virus "subclinically" about 1 in every 6 days. This "subclinical" shedding is generally greatest in the

"Herpes has become a major public health problem."

first six months after a person contracts the virus. The shedding rate declines slightly over the next six months and appears to fluctuate thereafter. Most people today with a first-time infection appear to have contracted it from sexual partners who were not aware of any symptoms. (Similarly, people with recurring cold sores in the mouth can transmit the virus between outbreaks.) "It's a tough message to have to tell people, but there's no 'safe' time [for people with the virus] to have [unprotected] sex," says one counselor at the National Herpes Hotline (919-361-8488).

The herpes virus can be devastating to newborns, as Barbara Wilkop of Birmingham, Michigan, knows too well. Her 10-year-old son, Jimmy, has an IQ of 35 as a result of contracting herpes from his mother at birth. Jimmy can hear, but he can't understand words. He can ride a bicycle, but he can't always figure out what to do at the end of a dead-end street. He has to be reminded to zip up his pants whenever he goes to the bathroom, and he has so little impulse control that at one family gathering he bit a cousin on the shoulder. "Sometimes I get so sad," says Wilkop. "Jimmy will never get a chance to drive a car, get married, buy a house, or see his first child born."

"Most people today with a first-time infection appear to have contracted it from sexual partners who were not aware of any symptoms."

About 1 in 3,000 infants nationally contracts the herpes virus during delivery, says David Kimberlin of the University of Alabama at Birmingham. Women who have had herpes for several years before having children rarely infect their infants during delivery, thanks to protective antibodies passed from mother to child in the womb. Only about 2 in 100 such infants pick up the virus during birth, and, in most instances, it infects only the skin, eyes, or mouth.

Infants at High Risk

But one third to one half of infants delivered to women who contract the virus for the first time late in their pregnancies contract herpes. In these cases, herpes often attacks the brain, causing death or severe neurological impairment, ranging from blindness and deafness to mental retardation. Because the consequences of infection can be so severe, obstetricians usually recommend delivery by Caesarean section if they spot even the hint of a lesion at the time of delivery. "The general rule is: 'No lesion, vaginal delivery; lesion, C-section,'" according to Larry Gilstrap, chairman of the committee on Obstetrics at the American College of Obstetricians and Gynecologists. As a result, genital herpes is one of the leading causes of C-sections nationally. Although precise figures are not available, Gilstrap estimates that herpes may be fourth or fifth on the list.

Doctors are debating whether pregnant women should be screened for herpes at their first prenatal visit to the doctor, as most are for syphilis, German measles, and a host of other diseases. Zane Brown of the University of Washington in Seattle contends that adding a blood test for herpes to the list makes good sense. "I can go from one end of a decade to the other and not see [a case of] syphilis or gonorrhea, but 35 percent of my patients have genital herpes," he says of his largely middle-class practice. It's especially important to identify high-risk couples, in which the man is infected and the woman isn't. Typically, he tells such couples to use condoms and prescribes for the men an antiviral drug, such as acyclovir or famciclovir, to suppress outbreaks and subclinical shedding, or he counsels couples to abstain from intercourse for the duration of the pregnancy.

Physicians who oppose prenatal screening for herpes argue that test results aren't that useful clinically. Even women who test positive in early pregnancy won't necessarily be shedding the virus during delivery,

> *"Despite the many health threats posed by herpes, few weapons are available to fight the disease."*

Gilstrap says. And a woman who tests negative at the start of her pregnancy could have picked up the virus by the end.

The opposition of many doctors to prenatal testing seems to stem from a reluctance to deal with the messy emotions that crop up after the diagnosis of an incurable disease—which herpes remains. One prominent obstetrician says that with herpes, "Ignorance is bliss. What am I supposed to say to a wife who tests positive and asks, 'Where did I get this from? I've only had relations with my husband'?"

There are dramatic reasons why all health care providers should deal with the topic. Besides inflicting health problems on infants, adults can find themselves in a fierce struggle with the virus. People with compromised immune systems are the most vulnerable. In burn victims, a herpes skin infection can spread bodywide. "Though rare, it's a well-recognized complication that can kill you," says University of Washington's David Koelle. Bone-marrow-transplant patients and people with lupus can succumb to herpes infections too, although hefty doses of antiviral drugs usually will keep the virus in check. Most AIDS patients—particularly in the disease's early stages—have sufficiently intact immune systems that lesions stay localized. But outbreaks can become the size of silver dollars or larger and be slow to heal.

Public-health experts are deeply concerned about studies finding that getting herpes sores puts sufferers at a much greater risk of contracting HIV—up to nine times as great—by providing portals for HIV to enter the body. "Especially in inner-city populations [which have a high incidence of herpes], it's plausible that herpes is fueling the spread of HIV," says Sharilyn Stanley at the National Institute of Allergy and Infectious Diseases (NIAID) in Bethesda, Maryland.

Despite the many health threats posed by herpes, few weapons are available to fight the disease. The diagnostic tests commercially available today are unreliable. People with active lesions can have them swabbed and cultured, but such "viral culture" tests are accurate only when lesions are newly formed and teeming with virus particles. Because many people don't get in to see their doctors until their blisters are partly healed, about half the herpes-infected people who take the test are falsely assured that they don't have the virus.

Testing the Blood

Doctors can give patients with no current symptoms a blood test for antibodies to HSV. But the tests currently on the market can't diagnose a case of genital herpes because they don't distinguish between HSV-1 and HSV-2. An accurate, reliable blood test that can tell HSV-1 from HSV-2 is being reviewed by the Food and Drug Administration, however, and may be available by early next year.

Several studies of couples in which one person is infected and the other isn't have shown that transmission is not inevitable, even after years of sexual contact—although often it takes only a few months for the uninfected partner to catch the virus. Herpes is a "very serious infection," according to Penelope Hitchcock, chief of the division of Microbiology and Infectious Diseases at NIAID, but "[it] is not the most infectious disease in the world."

Still, there is no reliable way to prevent transmission of the virus. Condoms provide only partial protection because the virus can be shed from parts of the body not covered by condoms. "Condoms work pretty well for HIV [which is found in body fluids], and not so very well with HSV," says Andre Nahmias of Emory University School of Medicine in Atlanta. Until recently, researchers hoped that nonoxynol-9, a spermicide often used with condoms and diaphragms, would prove to be an effective chemical barrier, wiping out virus particles as handily as it does sperm cells. But recent studies have shown that nonoxynol-9 is so irritating to the mucosal membranes of the female genital tract that it may increase a woman's susceptibility to infections by damaging these protective membranes. "This is the frustration of clinicians," says Nahmias. "What do you tell people to do?"

> *"If a person is not in a monogamous relationship with an uninfected person, he or she should always use condoms."*

To reduce the risk of contracting herpes, Hitchcock of NIAID recommends a few sensible precautions. If a person is not in a monogamous relationship with an uninfected person, he or she should always use condoms. If one partner carries the virus, the couple should never have sex when the partner has lesions, and they should use condoms at other times. If a partner has recurring lip sores, unprotected oral sex should be avoided. Women should abstain when they have vaginal yeast or bacterial infections, which can wipe out healthy microbes.

NIAID has begun funding a host of research projects aimed at developing new tools for stemming the epidemic. A promising area of inquiry is whether daily doses of acyclovir can help carriers of genital herpes protect their partners and infants from infection. A preliminary study published last year by Laurie Scott, then of the University of Texas Southwestern Medical Center in Dallas, and her colleagues suggests that women may be able to protect their babies from infection by taking acyclovir during the last month of pregnancy. Similarly, a study by Anna Wald and colleagues last year showed that acyclovir therapy reduced viral shedding between outbreaks in women by 94 percent. Wald says, "The transmission study hasn't been done yet, but these results do suggest that the drug may interrupt transmission [between sexual partners]."

Many herpes experts say that only a safe, effective vaccine will be able to decrease the number of people infected each year. But while many potential vaccines are being developed, all are at least a decade away.

Rates of HIV Infection Are Increasing Among Gay and Bisexual Men

by Cheryl Hawkes

About the author: *Cheryl Hawkes is a contributor to* Maclean's.

A member of the so-called safe-sex generation, Richard is a gay man in his 30s who became sexually active during the early part of the AIDS epidemic. From the start, he says, he always insisted on condoms, always approached sex 'with latex and a level of caution that seemed ill-matched with the excitement of the event.' But occasionally Richard (not his real name) took a chance and had unprotected sex. And with every blood test that came back HIV-negative, he felt bolder. 'Every year, the number of episodes would be more than the year before,' he admits. 'I guess I was rolling the dice.' Three months ago, Richard's luck ran out: his blood tested positive for HIV, the virus that causes AIDS.

He's not alone. Researchers across North America report that after years of declines, infection rates of HIV among gay men once again are climbing. What's more, the bulk of the new infections are among gay men 35 to 45 years old, men who have seen the worst of the AIDS epidemic and who should know how to avoid infection. 'Certainly I've lost a lot of friends over the past 15 to 20 years,' says Richard. 'I have a lot of friends who are HIV-positive. It wasn't as if I was unaware by any stretch.'

Infection Rates Increase

A study released earlier this month by University of Toronto researchers reported HIV infection rates among gay and bisexual men in Ontario have increased nearly 2 1/2 times since 1996, largely among men living in Toronto and Ottawa. The study looked at a provincial database of about 270,000 people of both sexes who had repeated HIV blood tests between 1992 and 1999. It then examined changes in results for each risk group. Among gay and bisexual men,

Reprinted from Cheryl Hawkes, "The Cost of Complacency," *Maclean's*, July 31, 2000. Reprinted with permission from *Maclean's*.

the infection rate went from less than one per cent of those tested (0.87 men per 100 tested) to 2.07 per cent by the end of 1999.

The U of T findings mirror similar reports from researchers in San Francisco, generally considered ground zero for trends in the AIDS epidemic. There, HIV infection rates among gay and bisexual men seeking anonymous testing have nearly tripled since 1997, after several years of decline. Another San Francisco study by a group called STOP AIDS reported that the proportion of men who said they 'always' use a condom fell to 60.8 per cent in 1997 from 69.9 per cent in 1994. Sixty-eight per cent of those who engaged in unprotected sex with a range of partners said they did not know the HIV status of all their partners.

The reasons for the increases are complex. They range from the misconception among young gay men that AIDS is an old person's disease to the impact of the so-called drug cocktails built around protease inhibitors. AIDS deaths in Canada fell by 32 per cent in 1996, the year the drugs were introduced, and by 70 per cent in 1997. There is also a sense of fatigue towards safer sex practices among older men. 'It's really difficult for anybody to maintain perfect behaviour 100 per cent of the time,' says Richard.

University of Toronto sociologist Dean Behrens has seen evidence of an increase in 'barebacking'—anal sex without a condom—over the past year or two. 'It's everywhere,' he says, citing Internet chat rooms and 'coverage in the gay media that almost normalizes the behaviour.' Behrens, who teaches courses on the sociology of AIDS says regular HIV testing can work against safe sex, reinforcing risky behaviour. 'You take some risks, you get tested and you're negative,' he says. 'So the next time you take more risks. It gives people a false sense of security.'

> *"HIV infection rates among gay and bisexual men seeking anonymous testing have nearly tripled since 1997."*

Ronald Johnson, associate executive-director of the Gay Men's Health Crisis in New York City, says community workers there are also seeing infection rates rising. 'A certain complacency about the epidemic has set in,' says Johnson, who is 52 and HIV-positive. Last year, his agency surveyed some 5,000 gay men about their safe-sex practices. 'We found higher rates of condom use than we were expecting. But we also saw more nuances around high-risk behaviour, more decisions made based on someone's status. It used to be that you assumed the other person was positive and practised safe sex. Now you assume the person is negative. We need to find out why this is.'

False Optimism

Drug cocktails may have given uninfected gay men a sense of false optimism. Despite intensive efforts, researchers still have not developed a vaccine for AIDS, and there is still no cure for the disease. Behrens points to pharmaceutical ads in U.S. magazines aimed at the gay and HIV-positive communities—magazines like *The Advocate* and *POZ*—that put the best face on anti-viral drugs. Yet anti-viral drugs do not work for 30 per cent of HIV-positive people, he notes. 'Of the rest, half will become resistant within three years. There is also an increase in infections with drug-resistant strains of HIV.'

> *"Drug cocktails may have given uninfected gay men a sense of false optimism."*

Charles Roy, executive-director of the AIDS Committee of Toronto, notes that anti-viral therapy for many can be a gruelling existence. In the past year, he says, one friend suffered a massive stroke and another had triple-bypass surgery due to the strain of the drugs. Diabetes rates are soaring among HIV-positive people, he says, and chronic diarrhea and nausea are common. There are also the telltale signs of lypodystrophy—a redistribution of fat in the body. 'It's no picnic. Yet what gets communicated to the average Joe is: the death rate is down and the drugs keep you alive.'

For Roy, the recent rise in HIV infection rates stems from deeper psychological issues. Older gay men, he says, 'have experienced so much loss in life. It's like I just want to be close to someone, to love someone and be loved back. These are powerful feelings that can overwhelm and lead to irrational behaviour.' Prevention messages, says Roy, need to be 'more hard-hitting, more in-your-face' and convey to HIV-negative men what it's really like to live with the virus.

Meanwhile, Richard plans to practise safe sex in the future; but not so safe as to inform every partner that he's HIV-positive. 'Anyone in the year 2000 who is basing their behaviour on the assumption that the other person has the responsibility,' he says, 'is engaging in just as much risk as I did.'

AIDS Is a Serious Problem in Africa

by Brian O'Reilly

About the author: *Brian O'Reilly is on the Board of Editors at* Fortune *magazine.*

At a trade show in Botswana, one of the most prosperous countries in Africa, a well-dressed crowd gathers to celebrate. The party, hosted by the De Beers-Botswana diamond monopoly, has attracted the nation's best and brightest: Miss Botswana Universe, business leaders, government ministers. They sip chardonnay and chatter with the aplomb of Manhattan socialites. In conversation, a television anchor calmly dismisses the extent of the AIDS epidemic in Botswana and disputes whether HIV even causes AIDS. Amid the good cheer, a jarring thought intrudes: Half the people in the room will probably be dead in five years.

The HIV/AIDS epidemic moving through Africa is unlike any plague the world has ever seen. It is bigger: More than 25 million Africans have already contracted the virus that will kill them within a decade; millions more will die in decades to come. It is crueler: Most epidemics decimate a population with frightening but merciful swiftness. This one travels in slow motion, hiding in its victims for years before they die slowly and painfully—but spreading all the while. And it is wreaking economic devastation in ways that epidemics rarely do, by attacking not the weak, the young, and the elderly, like most plagues, but killing off the most productive people in Africa: the well educated, the prosperous, the powerful, the parents of young children.

Denial

Although AIDS will claim many more victims than the medieval Black Death, which killed 20 million, Africa is in denial about the disease. Whole governments are struck dumb, unwilling to acknowledge the cause and extent of AIDS, and paralyzed by a lack of resources to fight it. The disease is strangely silent, almost underground. You don't see emaciated victims on city sidewalks in Botswana, South Africa, or Zambia. The people who return to

Excerpted from Brian O'Reilly, "Death of a Continent," *Fortune*, November 13, 2000. Reprinted with permission from *Fortune*.

their villages to die don't tell their families why they are sick. Wives don't admit that their husbands died of AIDS, and vice versa. Nurses at a small, tidy hospital near the gold mines west of Johannesburg say they have treated just 38 cases of AIDS among the 26,000 miners—even though miners have one of the highest HIV infection rates of any group in South Africa.

"Africa will never be the same," says Clem Sunter, an executive director of Anglo American, South Africa's gold and diamond mining colossus. "We don't know yet what the social and economic consequences will be, but AIDS will define the shape and structure of society in Africa. It is the biggest thing, bar none." Yet in South Africa, says Sunter, the silence on the subject is so great that "you can hear that proverbial pin drop."

AIDS lurks in rank back alleys and in plushly carpeted bedrooms; in thousands of grass-hut villages, where parents sell their last cow to raise money for a dying son or daughter; in hundreds of corporate boardrooms, like the one where eight of 12 top executives are HIV positive; in national parliaments, like Malawi's, where more than a dozen ministers have died; in the armies of Angola and Congo, where, according to the CIA, half the soldiers are HIV positive; in Lusaka, the capital of Zambia, where a TV ad promotes funerals for young and old!; in Uganda, where coffins with see-through portholes are pulled along the streets behind bicycles.

Stupefying Statistics

The statistics are stupefying. Africa, with just 11% of the world's population, is home to almost 75% of the people with AIDS. In Botswana, a Texas-sized country that borders South Africa, a United Nations report says 35% of men and women between 15 and 50 are HIV positive; if the infection continues to spread at its current rate, a 15-year-old Botswanan boy will have an 85% chance of dying of AIDS. South Africa, with by far the largest economy in Africa, has more HIV-positive people than any country in the world—about four million. (Except where noted, the statistics in this viewpoint are from the United Nations or the U.S. Agency for International Development—USAID).

Ironically, apartheid shielded South Africa from the epidemic. For years the country was isolated politically and economically by a global boycott protesting its treatment of blacks. When apartheid ended in 1991, South Africa's borders became more porous,

> *"More than 25 million Africans have already contracted the virus that will kill them within a decade."*

trade with its neighbors resumed, and HIV exploded. Barely 1% of the country's adult population was infected ten years ago, vs. nearly 20% today. The economic boom that came with the end of apartheid is now in serious jeopardy. Other African countries, already among the world's poorest, are seeing AIDS devour modest gains in life expectancy and economic growth.

Not all of the continent is suffering. The disease is rare north of the Sahara, where less than 1% of the population is HIV positive. In Africa's western bulge, around Senegal and Liberia, only about 3% are infected. More conservative sexual practices in the mostly Muslim northern countries and a less contagious form of HIV in western Africa may explain the lower rates.

Genocide by Mother Nature

By contrast, in a broad swath south and east of Lake Victoria, the rates are hideously high. The measure of devastation is not revealed in coarse economic statistics like GNP. The vast majority of Africans are subsistence farmers whose output doesn't even appear on macroeconomic radar. . . . AIDS in Africa, in other words, won't make a blip in your retirement portfolio.

Where it should be making a very large dent but mostly isn't—because the developed world is inured to suffering in Africa—is in our collective conscience. AIDS is genocide by Mother Nature, and it is killing a continent. For millions of families, the devastation is immeasurable. Because HIV attacks the immune system, a victim typically develops a series of debilitating diseases before dying. A farmer's ability to work is diminished, of course, but so is the entire family's, as his wife, children, and relatives spend more time caring for him and less time tending crops. A study by a farmers union in Zimbabwe reported that maize production dropped 61% after the death of a breadwinner. Cotton and vegetable production fell by half. Families that grow more lucrative but labor-intensive crops to sell to cooperatives or along the roadside often must revert to subsistence farming when the male adults become sick.

> *"If the infection continues to spread at its current rate, a 15-year-old Botswanan boy will have an 85% chance of dying of AIDS."*

Funeral expenses are large because the many friends and relatives obliged to attend must be fed. But the economic damage doesn't end with the funeral. Families desperate for a cure sell their most valuable assets to pay for treatment. The cattle go first, then the plow or the bicycle used to carry crops to market. "I know the family is on the brink of ruin when the bike or the plow get sold," says Jill Donahue, an American working to make small-scale credit available in Zambia. Even healthy farmers can be haunted by AIDS when their children move to cities to seek more opportunities, contract the virus, then return to their parents' village for care. "In Botswana, we go home to die," says Prisca Tembo, an AIDS prevention worker in the capital city of Gaborone.

In the course of impoverishing itself, a family frequently enriches people with virtually no modern medical skills. Traditional healers treat 70% of AIDS cases in Botswana. They charge $10 to $20 per visit to patients whose yearly income might be $500. For that they offer prayers and burn incense, or suggest that a victim cure his AIDS by having sex with a virgin. "If you want to get rich, come to Botswana as a traditional healer," says Karen Sorensen, a Lutheran missionary.

Benjamin Raletatsi runs an AIDS education center on the outskirts of Maun, a town of 35,000 in northern Botswana largely devoted to tourists viewing wildlife at the nearby Okavango Delta. Painted a cheery red, the center is near the riverbank, perhaps 500 dusty yards from the center of town, so visitors can come and go discreetly. Raletatsi says he urges AIDS

> *"AIDS is genocide by Mother Nature, and it is killing a continent."*

victims returning to their villages to tell their families the disease is incurable, though he admits that most parents would ignore the disclosure. Robert Clay, a USAID health official who specializes in fighting AIDS in Zambia, saw this firsthand when a woman in his office got sick. "Her parents did everything to save her, even flew her to Harare [in Zimbabwe] for treatment," says Clay. "Her mother told me, 'I've already lost four sons to AIDS. I'm not going to lose my daughter.'" The daughter died too.

Every family with AIDS is miserable, but each family is miserable in its own way. Take, for example, a woman married to a prosperous man who dies of AIDS. Even if she manages to avoid catching the disease from her husband, she is subjected to family rituals that condemn her to poverty and make her vulnerable to the virus. The dead husband's brothers often claim his property—his home, his savings, his life insurance, even death benefits from his employer. Although some countries have outlawed property grabs, tribal customs can be too strong for widows to resist. A widow must be "cleansed" by her husband's brothers to avoid becoming an outcast. "Cleanse" is a cruel word, for it means having sex with the husband's brothers to wash away his spirit. The brothers may refuse to perform the cleansing until the widow hands over all her property.

Sometimes a widow is assigned to a brother and cared for as a spare wife, but not always. One of the saddest scenes in Africa is the women sitting by the roadside in Lusaka, pounding rocks with a hammer. They collect the rocks from a nearby field, then break them into coarse gravel. If they are fortunate, a contractor may come by and buy the gravel for a few cents, to mix with cement. Many of the women appear to be starving.

Orphans

In families with young children, AIDS causes its own special problems and heartbreak. First, the father dies. A year or two later, the mother dies, having caught the virus from her spouse. They leave a handful of orphans who, maybe, can move in with grandparents. But the grandparents have often spent their savings on their dying son or daughter. At a time when they were counting on their children to support them in their old age, they instead have grandchildren to feed. Many such families face starvation. Even orphans taken in by relatives who can feed them have bleak futures. Zimbabwean orphans are half as likely to finish school as other children, mainly because their foster parents can't afford the minuscule school fees.

Africa's orphan problem is immense. The United Nations estimates that there are 13 million. David B. Dunn, the U.S. ambassador to Zambia, says that more than 25% of Zambia's children are orphans. The number is rising fast in the slums of South Africa. Driving through the rutted, narrow streets of Alexandra, a township on the outskirts of Johannesburg, health worker Linda Twala points out small hovels. "Six children in there. No parents. Four children in that one." Some youngsters eke out a living making trinkets to sell by the roadside, but often the girls become prostitutes, catching and spreading HIV, and the boys become petty criminals.

As a pediatrician in Zambia, Mutinta Nyumbu watched as AIDS invaded her country more than a decade ago. Now it has invaded her home. "I got a call yesterday from my cousin that another cousin had just had an AIDS-related stroke. He has eight children. I am already caring for my three sisters and their children. All their husbands have died of AIDS. How can I care for eight of my cousin's children? I just learned about this yesterday. I can't stop thinking about it." Other workers at her Lusaka health center have similar problems. "I've lost 20 relatives to AIDS," says Andrew Mlewa. "Now it's hitting my dad. He divorced my mom and married another woman. She died, her kids died. I have to drive eight hours to see him."

> *"More than 25% of Zambia's children are orphans."*

Risky Sexual Practices

Certain sexual practices have hastened the spread of AIDS. African men often demand "dry sex," claiming that a dry vagina is more pleasurable. The women are forced to use herbs and other means to dry themselves, but dry sex results in vaginal tears and abrasions that increase the rate of HIV transmission. Most men in eastern and southern Africa are uncircumcised, which seems to make them more vulnerable to HIV. Africans also have high rates of untreated syphilis, gonorrhea, and other sexually transmitted diseases, increasing by 20-fold their chances of catching HIV.

Condom use is rare; a Zambian survey found that only 6% of people reported using a condom in their last encounter with a spouse or live-in partner. Nils Gade, head of the Society for Family Health, a nonprofit organization in Zambia that distributes condoms, says Africans know, intellectually, that unprotected sex leads to AIDS. "If you quiz them on it, 95% of their answers are correct," says Gade. "But their behaviors don't change. It's like talking to teenagers about smoking. They know it kills, but they do it anyway." Gade says attitudes are changing, but slowly. "Ten years ago when our workers went into bars and tried to distribute condoms, they got thrown out. People would say there was no such thing as AIDS. Now they know."

Many men take young girls as partners, assuming they are less likely to have the virus than older, more sexually active women. Other men believe they will cure their own HIV by having sex with 100 virgins; they claim the virus is passed on to the girls. A survey of 1,600 children in Lusaka found that 25% of 10-year-old girls in poor sections of town had had sex, and 60% of 16-year-old girls. In countries where sex with young girls is most prevalent—Zambia, Botswana, Zimbabwe—overall rates of HIV are far higher.

> *"[Some] men believe they will cure their own HIV by having sex with 100 virgins."*

Well-educated, well-paid men are at particularly high risk for AIDS. They can afford to give clothes and a cell phone to a girlfriend in exchange for sex, to pay a prostitute, or to set up a mistress in an apartment. Men in authority can often demand sex from powerless underlings. The AIDS rate among schoolteachers, who are mostly male, is astoundingly high. About 85% of the teachers who died during the past few years in the Central African Republic were HIV positive. The reasons aren't entirely clear, but it appears that many demand sex from the children or their mothers in lieu of fees. Because women tend to be less educated than men and much less likely to have a job, it doesn't take much wealth to buy or barter for sex. A South African truck driver making $400 a month is rich to local women who don't earn that much in a year. Men from Mozambique and Tanzania leave their families to work in South African mines. Bored, lonely, and well paid, they spend their money on prostitutes.

Educated women appear to be just as much at risk as their male counterparts. They, too, are mobile and can travel and party in ways poor rural women cannot. "This is a very materialistic society," says a black American woman who has worked in Johannesburg for many years. "Two men I know were told by their girlfriends that their cars weren't good enough, that if the men didn't get new cars, they would leave." In Zambia, educated women past their teens are three times more likely to contract HIV than uneducated ones. . . .

Ineffective Government Response

The governments of some of the countries most affected by AIDS have been alarmingly inert, even counterproductive, in attacking the problem. By far the worst offender is Thabo Mbeki, President of South Africa. He claims to have personally investigated the disease and doubts that HIV leads to AIDS. He questions whether AZT, one of the most useful medicines in slowing the progress of HIV, really works. (Nelson Mandela spoke out only once about the disease while he was President.) Partly as a result of Mbeki's foolishness, South Africa refuses to give AZT to pregnant women close to term—even though it greatly reduces the spread of HIV to newborns. Dr. Colin Eisenstein, medical director at Anglo Gold, the nation's biggest gold-mining company, is furious. "If there were a foreign army camped out on our border that we knew was going to kill 25 million people, we'd do something about it," he says.

In other African countries, civil servants work to educate people about AIDS, but top leaders are invisible, rarely speaking out in public and failing to convey a sense of urgency. Only in Uganda, perhaps the hardest-hit country in the world, has the President, Yoweri Musevini, led the charge. The prevalence of HIV in Uganda has actually declined over the past 20 years, from 15% to 8%. Miss Botswana Universe, Mpule Kwelagobe, is crusading against AIDS in her country. In Zambia, where government workers, foreign charitable organizations, and groups like the U.S. Agency for International Development have worked hard, there are signs of progress. In areas of Lusaka, the HIV rate among 15- to 19-year-olds has dropped sharply. Robert Clay, the USAID employee, says it's not clear whether rates will stay down as the youngsters become more sexually active, "but it's a beginning.". . .

A Maddening Dilemma

AIDS in Africa presents the rest of the world with a complicated, maddening dilemma. How do compassionate people even begin to help? Whom should they help first? The terminally ill suffering from painful AIDS-related infections? Orphans who face a life of Dickensian bleakness? Healthy people who need to be educated about how to avoid contracting the virus in the first place? Or should the U.S. and other rich countries allocate money to provide the expensive medicines, widely available in the West, that can delay the onset of symptoms for years?

Here's another question: Would any of it make a difference? The billions of dollars wealthy nations have spent on roads and dams and malaria eradication haven't changed the lot of the average African. If African men refuse to use condoms and continue to view women as nothing more than sexual objects, how much sympathy do they deserve? Or are they just as insensitive as men everywhere—and unlucky enough to have been born in a place where 100 variables have conspired to make AIDS so ruinous?

> *"South Africa refuses to give AZT to pregnant women close to term—even though it greatly reduces the spread of HIV to newborns."*

No large-scale solution to AIDS in Africa is possible until the continent's leaders acknowledge their plague and cheap medicine becomes widely available to fight it. In the meantime, there are some things ordinary people can do. Persuade your church to bankroll a village orphanage. Help young girls buy school uniforms and books so that they can attend class. Contribute to an organization that sends medical supplies to nursing stations. Travel to Africa; it needs the tourist dollars. After you've oohed and aahed at the wild animals, visit a U.S. embassy to ask which private and government agencies deserve help.

No matter what well-intentioned people do, the suffering in Africa will linger for decades. AIDS will not come close to killing everyone there, of course, but it is certain to prove more devastating than any epidemic in history. It's as mind-boggling as it is heart-wrenching that as the developed world races over the Internet into the third millennium, Africa is falling ever deeper into poverty and death from a pestilence right out of the Old Testament.

Fear of Sexually Transmitted Diseases Is Exaggerated

by Susie Bright

About the author: *Susie Bright is an author and editor of the* Best American Erotica *series.*

I've been doing some traveling this summer, and every place I visit I pick up the local paper and read every word, down to each classified ad. Of course, there are plenty of local scandals to shake my head at, but what's been steaming up my glasses this season are the endless sex-scare headlines—one wide-eyed, hand-wringing tract after another:

"Herpes: There's nothing you can do about it!"

"What you must tell your kids about sex before it's too late!"

"You may have a sexually transmitted disease—even if you've never had sex!"

You can read this stuff everywhere from the *Hartford Courant* to the *Honolulu Advertiser.* Why don't they just bundle the headlines into one big package:

"Sex makes you sick! Especially if you've never tried it!"

Scare Tactics

As usual, young people are used to spur grown-up fears. We are exhorted to talk to our children about our sexual concerns, but not to have the same kind of serious chat with our adult peers. We're advised to scare kids "straight" about fleshly temptation, following the model of those former junkies, with their stories and scars from prison, brought into classrooms to intimidate teenagers on the subject of drugs. In the end, we make them promise, preferably trembling, that they'll never, ever do _____.

I have serious doubts about using tactics like these to prevent substance abuse, but applying them to sex is absurd. Are we supposed to convince kids that they should never touch another human being? Is that the end goal? I'd rather share a birth experience with young people, or teach them how to care for a child, than have them witness some spectacle that shames unwed teenage moms. Or maybe, just for some feminist irony, I'd like to bring in a group of older men who've fathered babies by teenage girls and raised none of them. Let's hear all about the stigma of their pain and embarrassment! Let me know when *that* appears in the *L.A. Times.*

Actually, I don't want to put anyone else on the rack. What I'm really interested in is the possibility that one lover has sex with another and no one's health is compromised in the least. Frankly, *that's* the most common sexual experience. But do any of these fear-mongering "educators" have a plan for sexual maturity rather than eradication? Everyone knows sex between two people is a mixed bag—so what makes any of it worth the stumbling and disasters? How many of us would say that if we could take it all back, we'd rather have not been sexual at all?

Herpes Hysteria

Herpes hysteria is one of my special pet peeves, and I have some rebuttals to the recent media yipping. Let me provide some support for those who are still having sex—you few wild bandits out there.

Herpes: There's something you CAN do about it—and even if you don't, it's not the end of the world.

Herpes is epidemic, and that's not because several million people used the same soiled towel. Yes, *theoretically* you can get herpes without sexual contact, but you won't! You will get it as a result of fucking and sucking—just like everyone else. The only way to drastically reduce your risk for herpes is to use condoms. Period. If you refuse to do that, then shut up and accept the inevitable. Herpes sores don't shine out like neon lights, and an afflicted lover doesn't even have to be showing a sore to be contagious. A barrier method that prevents skin-to-skin contact is the only thing that's going to reduce your risk.

The herpes scare stories I read always make a big fuss about how condoms can "fail"—but if that's true, how come Trojan hasn't gone out of business? Condoms are a lot more reliable than tampons, napkins, coffee filters, Dixie cups and a lot of other everyday products I could mention, but you don't hear people raving about those numbers, do you?

> *"What I'm really interested in is the possibility that one lover has sex with another and no one's health is compromised in the least."*

The big problem with condoms is that when the media refuses to talk about sex in plain language, it can be hard to figure out how to use them. The young and inexperienced are at a real disadvantage unless someone takes them in hand (of course that's a nice way to learn, too). But I can tell any man in 10 seconds how to use condoms with ease: Buy a bunch of different kinds and masturbate with them until you find a kind you like. Great wankers make great condom artistes. There's no performance pressure—just figure out your pleasure and stock up. For a delightful "insider" experience, put a drop of lube inside the reservoir tip before you slide it on. Carry rubbers on your person. Have plenty around, like candy.

I've had it with whiners who complain about condoms! They're just mad they're not getting laid more often. Guys who know what they're doing with rubbers are a lover's dream come true. When you aren't worried about getting knocked up or sick, you can thoroughly enjoy being horny. End of story.

Is Death Lurking Behind Every Sexual Curtain?

Let's say you do have herpes. Well, welcome to the club that includes almost every sexually active person on the planet. It's not the end of the world, although it can be very annoying. The worst part is the dearth of public information and a prejudice that is particularly American. Those ads for the drug acyclovir (which relieves some herpes symptoms, but provides no cure) show preppy white people walking around in a platonic daze. The manufacturers are reassuring you that you, the herpes "sufferer," are not a slut just because you have this disease. To that extent, they're truthful. Herpes is absolutely banal, not reserved for any practice, lifestyle or ZIP code. Drugs or no drugs, and individual exceptions notwithstanding, this is not a "crippling disease."

> *"The herpes scare stories I read always make a big fuss about how condoms can 'fail'—but if that's true, how come Trojan hasn't gone out of business?"*

I got infected during the most sexually monogamous period of my life—in middle age, not my torrid youth. I'm sure I'd been exposed before, but the virus got me at a time in my life—while I was raising a baby—when my body was sorely run down. For me, herpes outbreaks don't even include external manifestations: I just get flu-like symptoms of fatigue and achy limbs. Keeping the virus at bay, in my case, is more about nutrition, rest and other good health practices than it is about anything particularly sexual.

Here's what I'm telling kids—or anyone who will listen—about sex this summer: Sexual pleasure, intimacy and self-preservation are a beautiful combination, and they are well within anyone's reach. Don't be freaked out by stories that paint death lurking behind every sexual curtain. That's a cold lie. Our erotic lives are not only what our bodies are made for, they are also where our minds will inevitably take us. Sexual practice is indeed a sharing of the most tender parts of our bodies, and that's always going to be a risky proposition.

AIDS-Related Illnesses and Deaths Can Be Explained by Other Factors

by Peter Duesberg

About the author: *Peter Duesberg is a professor of molecular and cell biology at the University of California at Berkeley and a leading critic of current HIV/AIDS medical orthodoxy.*

Virtually everyone's life has been directly impacted by the drug-use epidemic—the only new health risk of the Western world since World War II. Most people in the industrial world either have tried an illicit drug or know others who have. Just one or two generations ago, high schools spent their time trying to control cigarette smoking in the rest rooms; in those same rest rooms today, students can find a laundry list of recreational drugs for smoking, swallowing, snorting, or even injecting.

The 1960s gained the reputation as the decade of freely available drugs, especially marijuana and psychedelics. But in reality, the widespread escalation in drug use began largely during the Vietnam War, about a decade before the appearance of AIDS. Much of the explosion has taken place only in recent years. Overall drug arrests in the United States totaled approximately 450,000 in 1980, according to the Bureau of Justice Statistics, and the total was up to 1.4 million by 1989. . . .

Naturally, one might expect major health problems in the wake of this drug explosion. If the timing of the AIDS epidemic—following on the heels of the drug epidemic—was no coincidence, then one should also find the spread of AIDS following the spread of drug use.

Not only did the drug-use epidemic take off shortly before AIDS appeared, but it hit hardest among precisely the same risk groups. The parallels are astounding. Both AIDS and drug use, for example, are concentrated in younger men. Between 1983 and 1987 the death rate among American men ages twenty-five to forty-four increased by about ten thousand deaths per year, the same as the average number of AIDS deaths per year in that time period. But also during the 1980s deaths from drug overdoses doubled in men of exactly the same ages, while deaths from blood poisoning—an indirect consequence of injecting drugs—quadrupled. During that same period, AIDS deaths sharply increased among New York injection drug addicts, as did deaths from blood poisoning or other pneumonias—both at exactly the same rate.

Ninety percent of all AIDS cases occur in men. But nine of every ten people arrested for possession of hard drugs are also male. Even the age distributions coincide perfectly. Men between the ages of twenty and forty-four make up 72 percent of AIDS cases, just as they make up 75 percent of people arrested or treated for use of hard drugs.

What can be said of drug use in the AIDS risk groups?

The fact that injection drug users make up one-third of American AIDS cases, more than 130,000 by the end of 1993, should give pause for thought. Consider how that number breaks down. This figure includes three-quarters of all heterosexual AIDS cases and more than two-thirds of all female AIDS cases. More than two-thirds of all babies with AIDS are born to mothers who inject drugs. Even 10 percent of the hemophiliac AIDS cases inject drugs. These statistics incorporate only self-reported drug injection, for they cannot confirm such illegal habits in people who will not admit to them. And more important, most drugs are inhaled or taken orally, not intra-venously. The Centers for Disease Control and Prevention (CDC), however, does not ask AIDS patients about nonintravenous drug use. It is more concerned about possible HIV contamination on the injection equipment—hence the "clean needle" programs. But heroin or cocaine itself is most likely more dangerous than the dirty needles through which it is passed.

> *"Not only did the drug-use epidemic take off shortly before AIDS appeared, but it hit hardest among precisely the same risk groups."*

AIDS and Fast-Track Homosexuals

The remaining AIDS cases occur mostly among male homosexuals, the group that originally defined the epidemic. But the homosexuals who get AIDS form a special subset—sexually hyperactive and often promiscuous men, the so-called fast-track homosexuals. Their lifestyle emerged during the 1970s together with the new drug-use epidemic in the bathhouses, discotheques, and sex clubs. These men accumulated hundreds or even thousands of sexual contacts within just a few years. Venereal diseases and exotic parasites spread like wildfire. Infectious diseases ranging from the flu to hepatitis B became commonplace, and heavy doses of antibiotics were taken by many each night before sex, just to prevent unsightly sores or acne.

Such extreme sexual activity cannot be done on a cup of coffee alone or even on natural testosterone. The fast-track lifestyle required liberal drug use—stimulants to get going, poppers to allow anal intercourse, downers to unwind afterward. Several drugs, combined with alcohol and marijuana, became par for the course of an evening, a routine that would go on for years. One homosexual man, a math professor in New York who has witnessed the fast-track scene, described the situation in a 1993 letter to Dr. Peter Duesberg. The letter is a testimony to the high-risk lifestyle behind AIDS:

> *"More than two-thirds of all babies born with AIDS are born to mothers who inject drugs."*

> From my experience in the New York City and Fire Island gay communities I can testify that more than a thousand (an ever increasing number) of my acquaintances have been diagnosed with HIV/AIDS over the past decade. Unfortunately some 250 (an estimate, it could be greater) of these are now prematurely dead. . . .

> I have a list of my friends and acquaintances who died under the HIV/AIDS diagnosis. There are 150 names on the list. . . . The remarkable thing about the people on this list and the hundreds of people living with an HIV diagnosis who presently come in and out of my life, sometimes daily, sometimes weekly, is that they almost all have a drug (recreational and medical) use and an alcohol use history of duration of often more than ten years. . . .

> Most of the people on my list abused some, if not all, of the following drugs used recreationally: alcohol, amylnitrite, barbiturates, butylnitrite, cocaine, crack, ecstasy (XTC), heroin, librium, LSD, Mandrex, MDA, MDM, mescaline, methamphetamine, mushrooms, PCP, purple haze, Quaalude, Seconal, special K, THC, tuinol, and Valium.

> Most of the people on the list hosted many diseases and some of these diseases more than once. The following microbial diseases or microbes were common: *Candida* albicans, chlamydia, cytomegalovirus, cryptosporidiosis, Epstein-Barr virus, gonorrhea, giardia, hepatitis A or B or C or D, herpes simplex (both 1 & 2), herpes zoster, gay bowel syndrome, scabies, venereal warts, and other parasites. In almost all of these cases the diseases were contracted before an HIV+ diagnosis.

> I know that my acquaintances ingested large amounts of various antibiotics, antifungals, and antiparasitics. Some used antibiotics before going out for sex as prophylaxis against sexually transmitted diseases. These antibiotics were routinely given to them by gay doctors familiar with the fast-lane scene. Of course, after HIV diagnosis the overwhelming majority of these people used antibiotics, antifungals, antivirals (AZT, ddI, ddc, d_4T, acyclovir, ganciclovir, etc.), as a matter of course, in various combinations over varying intervals of time. . . .

At gay discos, both in New York City and on Fire Island, the use of recreational drugs is prevalent. The most common drugs are cocaine, ecstasy, poppers, and special K. On weekends on Fire Island drug dealers hawk their goods on the beach and on the walks as well as announce their hotel room numbers. Drug consumption among the fast-track gays is "de rigueur."

I emphasize that my remarks on drug usage are my observations or they were related directly to me by the individuals involved. They are not judgments. . . .

As a result of these observations I am inclined towards the Duesberg drug-AIDS hypothesis. . . .

Larry Kramer, the volatile homosexual rights and AIDS activist who founded the AIDS Coalition To Unleash Power (ACT UP), has himself criticized the excesses of "fast-track living." A playwright and author by profession, he used his 1978 novel *Faggots* to lament the emptiness of anonymous homosexual activity. His book described the intense sexual promiscuity in the bathhouses, a lifestyle that could never be separated from the endless drug use on which it depended. . . . Years passed before AIDS forced the homosexual community as a whole to acknowledge Kramer's point.

Medical Research

Medical physicians and researchers have also described the drug problem rampant among many homosexuals. A surprising guest editorial appeared in a 1985 issue of the *Wall Street Journal*, cowritten by a journalist and a Washington, D.C., doctor, Cesar Caceres. The two authors cited official CDC AIDS statistics, as well as Caceres's own patients, to argue that drug use was so universal among AIDS patients that HIV could not be considered the syndrome's primary cause. AIDS patients, they protested, have "pre-existing immune damage" from years of drug use, without which AIDS cannot occur. In a direct challenge to the AIDS research establishment, they rhetorically asked, "Since drug abuse can severely damage the immune system, why has AIDS been identified primarily with sex, especially sex among homosexuals?"

> *"Since drug abuse can severely damage the immune system, why has AIDS been identified primarily with sex, especially sex among homosexuals?"*

Joan McKenna, an AIDS therapist from Berkeley, California, described similar drug use patterns among one hundred homosexual men in her medical practice: "We found . . . nearly universal use of marijuana; a multiple and complex use of LSD, MDA, PCP, heroin, cocaine, amyl and butyl nitrites, amphetamines, barbiturates, ethyl chloride, opium, mushrooms, and what are referred to as designer drugs."

John Lauritsen and Hank Wilson noted that "Leaders of People With AIDS

(PWA), who have known hundreds of PWA's, state that most of them were heavily into drugs, and all of them used poppers," and that the owner of a prominent homosexual sex club in New York candidly admitted, "I really don't know anybody who's had AIDS who hasn't used drugs."

Large-scale studies of fast-track homosexual volunteers confirm these descriptions. An early CDC study, interviewing more than 400 homosexual men recruited from venereal disease clinics, counted 86 percent of them as using poppers frequently. Another study of 170 such men found that 96 percent admitted inhaling poppers regularly, while most had also used cocaine, amphetamines, lysergic acid, and methaqualone; many had also taken phenylcyclidine, ethyl-chloride, barbiturates, and heroin. A study of more than 350 homosexual men from San Francisco discovered that more than 80 percent used cocaine and poppers, with a majority simultaneously consuming other hard drugs. And a similar Boston study of more than 200 HIV-infected homosexual men revealed that 92 percent inhaled poppers and 75 percent used cocaine, in addition to the usual laundry list of drugs. Among male homosexual AIDS patients, more than 95 percent typically admitted to popper inhalation; by comparison, fewer than 1 percent of all heterosexuals or lesbians used poppers. In these and other studies, HIV-positive men had always used more drugs than had uninfected men, and sexual activity was tightly linked to heavy drug use.

> *"In 1993, everyone of a group of 215 male homosexual AIDS patients from San Francisco reported the use of nitrite inhalants, in addition to cocaine and amphetamines."*

In 1993, everyone in a group of 215 male homosexual AIDS patients from San Francisco reported the use of nitrite inhalants, in addition to cocaine and amphetamines. Moreover, 84 percent of these men were on AZT. A parallel study from Vancouver showed in 1993 that virtually every male homosexual AIDS patient had used nitrites, cocaine, amphetamines, and AZT. Recreational drugs—including cocaine, amphetamines, and again AZT—were also the common denominator of all male homosexual AIDS patients from a group in Vancouver, Canada.

AIDS Babies and Drugs

Drugs have also brought babies into the AIDS epidemic. A small percentage of the total AIDS cases, infants tend to suffer from their own peculiar spectrum of AIDS symptoms such as bacterial infections and mental retardation. These symptoms read like the profile of "crack babies" and is no coincidence. In his book *And the Band Played On*, Randy Shilts revealed which babies were getting AIDS. "Whatever the homosexuals had that was giving them Kaposi's sarcoma and *Pneumocystis*," he noted ominously, "it was also spreading among drug addicts and, most tragically, their children." Except that these young victims did not get Kaposi's sarcomas, lymphomas, or various other diseases common to homosexual AIDS cases. Two-thirds of these children have had mothers who inject drugs; some large percentage of the rest have mothers snorting cocaine or otherwise using non-injected drugs. But only a few studies have reported identical syndromes among babies of drug-using mothers, regardless of HIV infection. . . .

Injection drug addicts, male homosexuals, and the children of drug-injecting mothers constitute 94 percent of all AIDS patients. Thus, the correlation between heavy drug use and AIDS is far better than between HIV and AIDS. Drugs are biochemically active, and hence psychoactive, every time they are taken—the reason for their popularity. But HIV is inert and dormant in persons with and without AIDS. And although thousands of HIV-free AIDS cases have been described in the medical literature, possibly indicating hundreds of thousands more, no study has ever presented a group of AIDS patients genuinely free of drug use or other AIDS risks such as hemophilia.

Taken together, these facts imply a central role for drug use in AIDS. But there are also experimental reasons to indict these drugs as causes of AIDS. Indeed, each of the major AIDS-risk drugs shows evidence of toxicity that could destroy the immune system or cause other AIDS diseases. . . .

> *"No study has ever presented a group of AIDS patients genuinely free of drug use or other AIDS risks such as hemophilia."*

Malnutrition, another potential AIDS risk factor, also plagues the drug addict, who spends money on drugs rather than on a complete diet. Protein and zinc deficiencies have been described among many drug users, but the nature and importance of these dietary problems has never been researched. In general terms, malnourished people do face a high risk of immune deficiencies and pneumonias. Protein- and vitamin-deficient diets are found in much of the Third World and existed throughout Europe immediately following the havoc of World War II. Under such conditions, opportunistic infections do run rampant.

If recreational drug use and its associated risks have produced 94 percent of the American AIDS epidemic, how can we explain the remaining 6 percent? Half of these extra AIDS victims caught HIV through blood transfusions, a point that fuels the popular belief in AIDS as a contagious disease. But a closer look at these patients reveals some surprising facts, ones that confirm AIDS is neither infectious nor a single epidemic. . . .

AIDS and the Blood Supply

Half of all blood recipients die within the first year after transfusion. Naturally, this risk does not apply equally to all patients. The very old, the very young, and the most severely injured bear the brunt of death. Transfusions, after all, are not given to *normal*, healthy people. These patients have undergone traumatic medical problems and require the blood transfusions to stay alive after risky surgery for cancer, bypasses, or hip replacements. In the case of an organ transplant, the patient is given special drugs designed specifically to suppress the immune system and thereby reduce the possibility of organ rejection. And the blood itself is foreign material, overloading an already-stressed immune system in proportion to the amount transfused.

> *"Each of the major AIDS-risk drugs shows evidence of toxicity that could destroy the immune system or cause other AIDS diseases."*

Transfusion recipients die of many complications, not the least being opportunistic infections that prey on weakened immune systems. . . .

Among AIDS patients, those who caught HIV through blood transfusions do not suffer Kaposi's sarcoma, dementia, or several other major diseases found in the homosexual or injection drug-using cases. Instead they develop the pneumonias and other conditions typical of such patients . . . with or without HIV. No evidence has shown that death rates from blood transfusions ever increased from HIV transmission, nor has anyone demonstrated that death rates declined again once the virus was screened out of the blood supply. One 1989 CDC study reported that among hundreds of transfusion patients, those with HIV died no more often than the uninfected during the first year—the official "latent period" between HIV infection and AIDS for such patients! In short, no new epidemic of disease has affected transfusion recipients in recent years, nor do their diseases belong under the same heading as AIDS in homosexual men or heroin addicts. . . .

Lacking key components that allow blood to clot, hemophiliacs have long faced poor prognoses. Depending on the severity of the disorder, any damage could potentially cause unstoppable bleeding, externally or internally. Hemophiliacs in the past constantly needed blood transfusions, which only added to the problem, although the difference could hardly be noticed against the background of early death. As recently as 1972, hemophiliacs had a median life expectancy of only eleven years.

Then an innovative product changed their lives permanently: Scientists invented a method of extracting from normal blood the proteins that hemophiliacs are missing. Known as *Factor VIII*, this blood component can be injected prophylactically on long-term schedules by hemophiliacs and restores most of the clotting ability they lack. Fewer hemorrhages are now occurring, and the median life expectancy has more than doubled, reaching twenty-seven years by 1987.

The clotting factor brings a price tag, and not just in financial terms. Where hemophiliacs once died from internal bleeding, they now gradually develop immune deficiencies as they get older. Commercial Factor VIII itself seems to be part of the problem: With or without HIV infection, hemophiliacs lose immune competence according to the cumulative amount of Factor VIII consumed.

However, when the clotting factor is highly purified, the immune system remains healthy. Cost, unfortunately, bars many hemophiliacs from using the purified Factor VIII. Hemophiliacs treated with commercial Factor VIII consequently develop some opportunistic infectious diseases in the long run, particularly pneumonia and yeast infections. Those with HIV, who are counted as AIDS cases, get these same pneumonias, while they are unaffected by the Kaposi's sarcoma, lymphoma, wasting disease, and dementia that afflict homosexuals or heroin addicts who have AIDS. And as would be expected if these hemophiliac diseases were not caused by HIV, those with hemophilia-AIDS are on average at least ten years older than the rest—ten extra years of clotting factor and blood transfusions.

Ryan White

Ryan White provides a case in point. The young Indiana teenager became a national symbol of heroic battling against AIDS after his school expelled him as a threat to the other students. His family's lawsuit eventually prevailed, and a court order forced the school to accept him back into the classroom. The ruling was based on the fact that HIV is difficult to transmit. The news media kept a periodic spotlight on White's life, and when he became sick and was hospitalized by 1990, the story splashed across the front pages as implicit proof the deadly virus could kill even the

"Malnutrition, another potential AIDS risk factor, also plagues the drug addict, who spends money on drugs rather than on a complete diet."

healthiest of people. White's death in April drew so much attention that entertainers Elizabeth Taylor and Michael Jackson attended his funeral. Although the news media portrayed the death as the tragic end to White's long fight with AIDS, the doctor never publicly confirmed that the death certificate actually attributed the cause of death to AIDS.

A phone call to the Indiana Hemophilia Foundation to check the details generated a very different story. A foundation representative directly familiar with White's case was asked of what specific AIDS diseases White died. Only internal bleeding and hemorrhaging, liver failure, and collapse of other physiological systems were listed. These conditions interestingly happen to match the classical description of hemophilia, none being listed as peculiar to the AIDS condition, but the representative did not seem to know that. It was then acknowledged that White's hemophilia condition was more severe than the average, requiring him to take clotting factor every day near the end. On top of all that, White had taken AZT, the former toxic cancer chemotherapy now prescribed as AIDS treatment. Hemophiliacs, needless to say, are particularly vulnerable to the internal ulcerations induced by such chemotherapy. Thus, only media hype transformed White's death from a severe case of hemophilia, exacerbated by AZT, into AIDS.

The Connection Between AIDS and AZT

Those hemophiliacs whose diseases are reclassified as AIDS tend to have the severest clotting disorders in the first place, needing more Factor VIII and transfusions to stay alive. On the other hand, hemophiliacs have less to worry about than ever before. Of the twenty thousand hemophiliacs in the United States, some three-quarters were infected by HIV through the blood supply a little more than a decade ago. Yet during that same time period, clotting factor doubled their life expectancies, and very few are diagnosed with AIDS each year. HIV has made no measurable impact on the well-being of hemophiliacs, except for those who are treated with the highly toxic "anti-HIV" drug AZT. . . .

Many HIV-positive people, whether they have symptoms or not, would normally not die of AIDS, but do so anyway. The reason lies in their treatment, AZT, one of the most toxic substances ever chosen for medical therapy. This drug is now creating a scandal that may soon explode as the most embarrassing in the history of medicine.

The Worst of the AIDS Crisis Has Passed

by Bruce Shenitz

About the author: *Bruce Shenitz is a New York City–based writer and editor who writes about social and cultural topics.*

Sometimes no news really is good news. On August 13, 1998, the banner headline of San Francisco's *Bay Area Reporter* screamed in bright red ink, NO OBITS, when the paper received no AIDS-related death notices for an entire week—the first such nonoccurrence in 17 years. Michael Bettinger, a San Francisco psychotherapist with a large gay practice, remembers that "a surprising number of clients brought in the paper to talk about it." After 15 years, during which death had become commonplace and expected, he says, the no-obits issue was "noted as a marker."

After more than a decade of perpetual loss and mourning, the atmosphere in gay neighborhoods has changed. No longer do most gay men view everything through the filter of HIV. More and more, AIDS is seen as a chronic, not fatal, disease. What was once the main focus of gay life is now just one of many issues that occupy gay men.

The AIDS Crisis Is Over

Though the initial excitement over the new atmosphere produced a backlash from AIDS service groups warning against a premature rush to judgment, the most succinct summation of the current moment still comes from gay sex advice columnist Dan Savage, who wrote in February 1997 that "even if AIDS ain't over, the AIDS crisis is." While AIDS practitioners and social service providers differ on what should happen next, most agree that we have entered a new chapter in the history of the disease, one that will pose new challenges—and may require very different approaches than in the past.

A dearth of newspaper obituaries is not the only sign of the change. For the first time since 1990, AIDS was not one of the ten leading causes of death, dropping from eighth place in 1996 to 14th in 1997. The National Center for

Reprinted from Bruce Shenitz, "The Worst Is Over," *The Advocate*, January 19, 1999. Reprinted with permission from the author.

Health Statistics (NCHS) at the federal Centers for Disease Control and Prevention (CDC) reported in October that HIV-related deaths fell 47% from 1996 to 1997. In 1998, 16,865 people died from HIV-related illness, compared with 31,130 in 1996. For the 25–44 age group, the decrease was even more dramatic: The disease is now only the fifth leading cause of death, down from the leading cause in 1995.

New treatments have played a key role in the drop, but the number of AIDS deaths was already trending down. Robert Anderson, a statistician at NCHS, points out that 1995 was the peak year for AIDS deaths and that the increase from 1994 to 1995 was very small. In some large cities the numbers peaked even earlier—Seattle in 1993 and San Francisco in 1992. These declines in the death rate reflected the success of prevention efforts during the 1980s, which resulted in lower rates of infection, which ultimately led to lower mortality rates.

Even as public health officials welcome the decline in mortality, they offer a more nuanced reading of what the news really means. Helene Gayle, director of the CDC's National Center for HIV, sexually transmitted disease (STD), and tuberculosis (TB) Prevention, has pointed out that "we may just be seeing a postponement of death. We want to be sure people understand these are not cures."

New Challenges

Robert Wood, director of the HIV/AIDS Control Program at the Seattle-King County Department of Public Health, notes that any interpretation of the new statistics should take into account the interplay between the incidence of new cases and the survival and mortality rates. In one commonly used model, says Wood, the total number of people living with AIDS can be thought of as a beaker of water; new cases of AIDS drip into the beaker through a pipe on top, while a valve at the bottom releases water from the beaker as people die of the disease. With new cases coming in at the top at approximately the same rate and the mortality rate declining, the number of people living with AIDS is growing—which has implications for public health and AIDS service policies.

While there may be fewer people living with AIDS who are homebound and need meals delivered, for example, more may need job counseling or other services as they go on to live longer with the disease.

> *"More and more, AIDS is seen as a chronic, not fatal, disease."*

With such challenges, keeping the news good won't be easy. Scott Hitt, chairman of President Clinton's Advisory Council on HIV/AIDS and an HIV specialist in Los Angeles, believes the decreased death rate won't be sustained without better access to health care. "Traditionally, we have not given good access to care for the groups getting infected," he says. "Youth, people of color, and women do not have the same access to care as middle-class men." More than half the new cases of HIV infection occur among African-Americans, even though they make up only about 13% of the U.S. population; AIDS is still the leading cause of death among African-Americans aged 25–44.

For those men who are HIV-positive, the change caused by dropping mortality rates is profound. "The shift is from dying with as much dignity and health as possible to living with minimum inconvenience," says Robert E. Penn, author of *The Gay Men's Wellness Guide*. For people who've experienced a sudden turnaround in health, that can mean a major adjustment. Michael Holtby, a licensed clinical social worker in private practice in Denver, says that people who "spent years preparing to die and went on disability now have to switch gears and think about going back to work."

Shifting Priorities

Of course, the emotional toll of the disease remains, even if it seems muted. For those who have not been helped by the combination therapies, says Michael Shernoff, a New York psychotherapist and editor of the book *Gay Widowers: Life After the Death of a Partner*, "it's hard to be magnanimous for those people for whom it's working." People who have improved with the new drugs but have already lost partners and friends often feel "an intense sadness that the people we loved didn't live long enough to benefit," Shernoff adds.

"For the first time since 1990, AIDS was not one of the ten leading causes of death, dropping from eighth place in 1996 to 14th in 1997."

And the challenges facing AIDS organizations have not lessened either. Some AIDS organizations have lamented that fund-raising is more difficult now that AIDS seems to be off the front burner. Eric Rofes, author of *Dry Bones Breathe: Gay Men Creating Post-AIDS Identities and Cultures* and a former executive director of San Francisco's Shanti Project, believes those problems underline how groups need to rethink their missions. "When medical treatments result in a resumption of 'normal life' for most people with HIV, maybe the mission of AIDS service groups should shift," he writes.

Rofes suggests that local AIDS organizations might broaden their mandate to serve a broader range of health concerns within the gay and lesbian community—including, for example, breast cancer care for lesbians. Or, Rofes adds, as middle-class white gay men become less central to AIDS, perhaps "gay men should simply relinquish ownership of the groups we founded in the 1980s." For many gay men, that's an idea that would have seemed inconceivable five years ago: to give up the disease that for so long seemed to define them.

AIDS Rates in Africa Are Exaggerated

by Tom Bethell

About the author: *Tom Bethell is the Washington, D.C., correspondent for the* American Spectator.

Hype about AIDS in Africa has reached new heights. Secretary of State Madeleine Albright and Vice President Al Gore (at the U.N. Security Council) have declared it to be an international security threat. AIDS is now called the leading cause of death in Africa, with over two million deaths last year, and the epidemic in sub-Saharan Africa is spreading "nearly unabated." Seventy percent of all AIDS cases are said to be African. On *Newsweek*'s cover we read of "10 Million Orphans." Meanwhile, in a "Tour of Light," a troupe of orphans from "devastated Uganda" performs on the Kennedy Center stage. There are calls for a new Marshall Plan.

Skepticism about what governments say—always scarce among journalists—vanishes completely when it comes to "plagues" and epidemics. At the mention of AIDS, newspaper stories are virtually dictated by public health officials. The *New York Times* is the pre-eminent example, with other publications trotting behind uncritically. A rare exception is the science journalist Michael Fumento, now with the Hudson Institute. Another is Charles Geshekter, a professor of African history at California State University at Chico. He has made 15 trips to Africa and has written widely about AIDS in that continent.

The author of *The Myth of Heterosexual AIDS*, Fumento told me that he found the recent reports of HIV infection rates of 25 percent in some African countries to be not believable. The alarmist predictions about the progress of AIDS in this country have not been borne out, he said. African AIDS is an attempt to find the bad news elsewhere. Here, AIDS has not spread into the general population, and never will. It has remained confined to the major "risk groups," mainly intravenous drug users and fast-lane homosexuals. But in Africa, more women than men are said to be infected with the virus. Professor

Reprinted from Tom Bethell, "Inventing an Epidemic," *The American Spectator*, April 2000. Reprinted with permission from *The American Spectator*.

Geshekter, too, sees African AIDS as a prolongation of the gravy train for public health experts. "AIDS is dwindling away in this country," he told me. "The numbers are down. What are the AIDS educators to do? Africa beckons."

Expanding Definitions

Here is an "African AIDS" primer. Over the years AIDS American-style was redefined more and more expansively. In 1993, for example, the Centers for Disease Control (CDC) in Atlanta added cervical cancer to the list of AIDS-defining diseases, with the unacknowledged goal of increasing the numbers of women. The overwhelming preponderance of males was an embarrassment to infectious-disease epidemiology, given that the viral agent was supposed to be sexually transmitted. AIDS is a name for 30-odd diseases found in conjunction with a positive test for antibodies to the human immunodeficiency virus. Being "HIV positive," then, is the unifying requirement for an AIDS case. Here is the key point that the newspapers won't tell you. To diagnose AIDS in Africa, no HIV test is needed. The presence of the unifying agent that supposedly causes the immune deficiency, the ID of AIDS, does not have to be established.

This was decided by public health officials at an AIDS conference in Bangui, a city in the Central African Republic, in October 1985. This meeting was engineered by an official from the CDC, Joseph McCormick. He wanted to establish a diagnostic definition of AIDS to be used in poor countries that lacked the equipment to do blood

> *"To diagnose AIDS in Africa, no HIV test is needed."*

tests. He also succeeded in persuading representatives from the World Health Organization (WHO) in Geneva to set up its own AIDS program. The appearance of sick people in Zaire hospitals had persuaded McCormick and others that AIDS now existed in Africa—this before HIV tests had even been conducted. And here was something important to write home about: Slightly more women than men were affected. Back in America, as Laurie Garrett wrote in *The Coming Plague*, McCormick told an assistant secretary of Health and Human Services that "there's a one to one sex ratio of AIDS cases in Zaire." Heterosexual transmission had been established. Now we were all at risk! AIDS budgets would soar.

The CDC had an "urgent need to begin to estimate the size of the AIDS problem in Africa," McCormick wrote in his book, *Level 4: Virus Hunters of the CDC*.

> Only then could we figure out what needed to be done—and where. This is what is known as surveillance. It involves counting the number of cases of AIDS. But we had a peculiar problem with AIDS. Few AIDS cases in Africa receive any medical attention at all. No diagnostic tests, suited to widespread use, yet existed. . . . We needed a clinical case definition—that is to say, a set of guidelines a clinician could follow in order to decide whether a certain person had AIDS or not. This was my major goal: if I could get everyone at the

WHO meeting in Bangui to agree on a single, simple definition of what an AIDS case was in Africa, then, imperfect as the definition might be, we could actually start to count the cases, and we would all be counting roughly the same thing.

The "Bangui Definition"

His goal was achieved. The "Bangui definition," was reached "by consensus." It has proven useful, McCormick added, "in determining the extent of the AIDS pandemic in Africa, especially in areas where no testing is available." Here are the major components of the definition: "prolonged fevers (for a month or more), weight loss of 10 percent or greater, and prolonged diarrhea." No HIV test, of course. What this meant was that many traditional African diseases, pandemic in poverty-stricken areas with tropical climate, open latrines, and contaminated drinking water, could now be called something else: AIDS.

The Bangui redefinition was published in CDC's Morbidity and Mortality Weekly Report, and in *Science* magazine, but you would be hard put to find it in our major newspapers. Take the *New York Times*, whose main AIDS reporter has long been Lawrence K. Altman. He is himself a former public health officer, and like McCormick worked for the CDC's Epidemic Intelligence Service. He wrote the first newspaper article on AIDS, in 1981, and in November 1985 wrote two huge stories for the *Times* on African AIDS. "To this reporter," he wrote in the first, "who is also a physician and who has examined AIDS patients and interviewed dozens of doctors while traveling through Africa, the disease is clearly a more important public health problem than many African governments acknowledge." The story filled an entire inside page of the paper, and it included a "box" on the Bangui meeting. It mentioned a "hospital surveillance system to determine the extent of AIDS," but Dr. Altman omitted to say that, in Africa, AIDS could now be diagnosed without an HIV test.

The obvious problem was pointed out by Charles Gilks in the *British Medical Journal* in 1991. Persistent diarrhea with weight loss can be associated with "ordinary enteric parasites and bacteria," as well as with opportunistic infection, he wrote. "In countries where the incidence of tuberculosis (TB) is high," as it is in Africa, "substantial numbers of people re-

> *"Many traditional African diseases, pandemic in poverty-stricken areas with tropical climate, open latrines, and contaminated drinking water, could now be called . . . AIDS."*

ported as having AIDS may in fact not have AIDS." By then, the *Times* had published another huge series on African AIDS, this one reported by Eric Eckholm and John Tierney. It emphasized the need for condom distribution in Africa ("since 1968, A.I.D. has given 7 billion condoms to developing countries") but the reporters again overlooked the relaxed definition.

Unlike dysentery and malaria, of course, plagues and epidemics reward reporters with front-page stories. And the budget requests of public health departments are met with alacrity. It was mutually convenient, surely, even if coincidental, that Altman and McCormick emerged from the same CDC intelligence service.

Is AIDS Running Rampant in Africa?

The loose definition has allowed health officials to conduct small surveys and make sweeping extrapolations to entire nations: AIDS is running rampant! Ten million orphans! (*Newsweek* might have told us that, in WHO lingo, an "orphan" is someone under 15 whose mother has died. With life expectancy short, and fertility rates high, it is to be expected that a lot of African children are still under 15 when their mother dies.)

> *"The loose definition [of AIDS] has allowed health officials to conduct small surveys and make sweeping extrapolations."*

In a forthcoming article, Michael Fumento comments on the vagueness of the Third World AIDS estimates, "made by organizations that are given more funds if they declare there's more AIDS." He adds:

> The Statistical Assessment Service [STATS] in Washington D.C. has noted recently that the World Health Organization in its latest ranking of the world's greatest killers dropped TB down the list while moving AIDS up. The best explanation, STATS director of research David Murray told me, is that WHO noted that many Third World AIDS victims also suffer from TB, that both AIDS and TB data are just educated guesses, and so felt justified in simply shifting a huge chunk of deaths out of the TB category into AIDS. He was unable to get anyone from the organization to comment.

That surely is what happened. The CDC added TB to its list of AIDS-defining diseases in 1993, and, with no need for an HIV test in Africa, TB falls under the "AIDS" umbrella. All along, incidentally, someone has been keeping a stricter tally of the AIDS cases actually reported to the WHO. The organization's Weekly Epidemiological Record (November 26, 1999) states that a cumulative total of 794,444 cases of AIDS in Africa has been reported to Geneva since 1982. "Anyone who wants to disprove those numbers should provide better, locally based figures," says Charles Geshekter of Cal State University. "So far, no one has."

In South Africa, which he visited recently, Geshekter found that HIV tests are conducted at prenatal clinics and the results extrapolated across the country. One problem is that pregnancy is only one of the many conditions that trigger a "false positive result." The reaction is not specific to HIV. Antibodies to many other endemic infections also trigger false HIV alarms. The problem has been well-known for 15 years, and it alone renders all African AIDS projections meaningless.

African Deaths Are Not Caused by AIDS

Yes, people are dying all over Africa. The continent's population, whether sub-Saharan or supra-, continues to climb rapidly all the same. People are not dying of AIDS but of the diseases that have always afflicted those parts of the globe where the water is not clean and sewage is not properly disposed of. Poverty, unclean water, and tropical weather make for insalubrious conditions. They have been exacerbated by civil war and the vast conflict raging in and around Central Africa. During his recent visit, Professor Geshekter asked a woman from a rural Zulu township what made her neighbors sick. She mentioned tuberculosis and the open latrine pits next to village homes. "The flies, not sex, cause 'running tummy,'" she said. Her understanding of public health would seem to be more advanced than that of the highly paid health officers who fly in from Atlanta and Geneva.

A sub-Saharan male-and-female AIDS epidemic implies that Africans have abandoned themselves to reckless sexual promiscuity. Recreational drug use is not alleged, and it is well established that it takes a thousand sexual contacts on average to transmit HIV heterosexually. (That is why HIV has stayed confined to risk groups in the West.) Fables of insatiable African truck-drivers and rampant prostitution—Beverly Hills morals imputed to African villagers—are attempts to rationalize the equal-gender epidemiology of AIDS

"People [in Africa] are not dying of AIDS but of the diseases that have always afflicted those parts of the globe where the water is not clean."

in Africa. Moslem countries to the north are less likely to accept this libel, so we may predict that the "epidemic" will remain firmly sub-Saharan. Cairo is a river's journey away from the Uganda hotbeds, and yet WHO reports a demure cumulative total of 215 cases in Egypt (pop. 65 million) since AIDS began.

Chapter 2

Who Is at Risk for Contracting Sexually Transmitted Diseases?

Chapter Preface

Black women are eighteen times more likely than Caucasian women to be infected with HIV, while Hispanic women are eight times as likely. Experts report that cultural attitudes are a major factor in the spread of the disease among these groups. How such cultural attitudes should be addressed to reduce AIDS infection has been a major dilemma.

Many of these women were infected through sexual contact with their male partners, who exposed the women due to their refusal to use a condom during sexual intercourse. Their refusal is largely cultural. According to Ian Smith, in an article for *Time* magazine, "Many young African Americans view [condoms] as a challenge to their manhood." Latin cultures place a strong emphasis on traditional sex roles. Women are expected to do what their partner wishes—engaging in intercourse without a condom, for example. In addition, these minorities often live in areas where AIDS education is inadequate; thus, they are less likely to take AIDS tests and prevent the further spread of the virus if they are infected. The inadequacy of the education also leads to dangerous misconceptions—some African American men consider AIDS to be a disease that affects white homosexuals and thus believe they can still safely engage in unprotected sex with their female partners.

These cultures are also marked by homophobia. Some African American and Hispanic women acquired the virus through their husbands or boyfriends, who were themselves infected through same-sex intercourse. However, the stigma placed on homosexuality makes these men loath to acknowledge their actions, placing their wives and girlfriends at further risk. Jacob Levenson notes that homosexuality is looked down upon in many black churches. Homophobia is also intense in Latino cultures; even the infected women frequently refuse to accept that their husbands might be homosexual or bisexual.

African American women and Latinas are two populations that are increasingly afflicted with sexually transmitted diseases. In the following chapter, the authors consider the risk of STDs among minorities and other vulnerable populations.

Promiscuity Increases the Risk of Sexually Transmitted Diseases

by Joe S. McIlhaney Jr.

About the author: *Joe S. McIlhaney Jr. is an obstetrician and gynecologist who specializes in infertility in Austin, Texas.*

Largely because of the heightened promiscuity of the past thirty years, America faces a health crisis: a silent epidemic of sexually transmitted diseases, also known as STDs. To be certain, venereal diseases are nothing new, but the increased variety of sexually transmitted diseases, not to mention the increased number of Americans who contract them, *is* new. In 1997 the Institute of Medicine not only claimed that "eight new sexually transmitted pathogens (germs) have been identified since 1980, bringing with them new challenges to prevention and treatment," but also warned that "more STDs will emerge and become established in the U.S." The warning was prophetic; shortly after the institute released its report, hepatitis C—approximately 20 percent of which cases are transmitted sexually—was recognized as a dangerous sexually transmitted disease that affects approximately four million Americans, most of whom do not know they are infected.

Not only are Americans contracting forms of sexually transmitted diseases that were unknown twenty years ago, but also such diseases are infecting increased numbers of Americans. For instance, 60 percent of sexually active females at a major university were found to be infected with human papillomavirus (HPV), the most common sexually transmitted disease in the United States. This sexually transmitted virus causes more than 90 percent of all precancer and cancer of the cervix, a cancer that kills about five thousand American women annually; condoms—the contraceptive device that some experts claim will insure "safer" sex—provide essentially no protection against HPV transmission. Genital herpes, another sexually transmitted disease, is also on

Reprinted from Joe S. McIlhaney Jr., "The Medical Downside for Unfettered Sexuality," *Family Policy*, September/October 1999. Reprinted with permission from Family Research Council.

the rise; the number of white teenagers infected by genital herpes during the past fifteen years has increased five-fold. In addition, HIV remains without a cure; approximately four hundred thousand Americans—as many as died in World War Two—have died from AIDs-related illnesses.

Promiscuity and Infection

More Americans contracting an increasing number of sexually transmitted diseases should come as no surprise, as Americans are engaging in sexual relations with more partners than they did twenty years ago. As the authors of the most comprehensive study of sexuality in America, conducted through the National Opinion Research Center at the University of Chicago, write in *Sex in America*: "The common perception is that Americans today have more sexual partners than they did just a decade or two ago. That, it turns out, is correct." The medical reality, however, is that the more sexual partners one has, the greater the risk of becoming infected with a sexually transmitted disease. The authors state: "The risk of STDs is increased by the total number of lifetime partners, whether over a short period of time or spread over a lifetime." Other researchers confirm these findings. Douglas T. Fleming, for example, discovered that 10.2 percent of persons who had only one sexual partner had genital herpes; of those with two to four partners, 20.7 percent had genital herpes; of those with more than fifty partners, 46 percent had genital herpes. In other words, the more sexual partners one has, the higher the risk of contracting herpes. The authors conclude: "Of the other demographic and behavioral factors assessed . . . , the strongest predictor of HSV-2 (genital herpes) infection was the lifetime number of sexual partners."

> *"More Americans contracting an increasing number of sexually transmitted diseases should come as no surprise."*

More than any other age group, America's teenagers are negatively impacted by sexually transmitted diseases. Not only are they physically more susceptible than adults, but many of them have multiple sexual partners. Twenty-five percent of all new cases of sexually transmitted diseases occur in teenagers, while two-thirds of all new cases occur in those between the ages fifteen to twenty-four years. Sexually transmitted diseases are so common in this latter group that a minimum of one-third of the sexually active will acquire a sexually transmitted disease by their twenty-fourth birthday, regardless of contraceptive use. This statistic is not surprising. When the Centers for Disease Control studied youth sexual activity, the center found that 58.1 percent of girls who lost their virginity by the age of fifteen reported more than five sexual partners when interviewed a few years later; only 11.3 percent of the girls had limited themselves to only one sexual partner. Of the girls who commenced intercourse by the age of sixteen, 44.7 percent reported more than five sex partners when interviewed later; only 18.6 percent reported only one partner. Among young women who had not engaged in sexual activity until after age twenty, however, only 15.2 percent reported more than five sexual partners while 52.2 percent reported one partner.

> *"Today's epidemic of sexual diseases appears to stem from a greater willingness of Americans to take risks in the sexual area of life."*

Based upon these studies, today's epidemic of sexual diseases appears to stem from a greater willingness of Americans to take risks in the sexual area of life, primarily by involvement with increased numbers of sexual partners. Why Americans, and especially American teenagers, continue to assume these dangerous health risks is not entirely clear. Whatever the reasons, these increased medical and health risks represent just another broken promise of a revolution that attempted to divorce sexuality from monogamous, heterosexual marriage and children.

African Americans Are Disproportionately Affected by AIDS

by Jacob Levenson

About the author: *Jacob Levenson is a writer for* Mother Jones.

Pastor Preston Washington is seated at a table with four other AIDS panelists at Canaan Baptist Church of Christ in Harlem. In front of him, bathed in pale fluorescent light, are more than 100 people from New York City's black church community. It's a Friday morning in early March 2000, and they have assembled around a dozen or so circular tables in a large, windowless meeting room to discuss the devastation AIDS is wreaking on African Americans. Washington feels tired; he and his staff have worked hard to coordinate their commencement breakfast for the national Black Church Week of Prayer for the Healing of AIDS.

Everyone who's gathered this morning has been handed the latest list of grim AIDS statistics from the Centers for Disease Control (CDC). The numbers are alarming: The virus is now the No. 1 killer of all African Americans between the ages of 25 and 44. Black women are 18 times more likely than white women to be infected with HIV. Fifty percent of the country's infected elderly population is black. Of all adolescent AIDS cases, 62 percent are African American. And in 1999, African Americans, who make up roughly 13 percent of the population, accounted for 54 percent of all new AIDS cases. What's equally disturbing, Washington knows, is that most members of these churches remain unaware of how deeply the epidemic has reached into their communities—and how close it has crept to their lives.

Standing at a lectern to Washington's left, his friend, the Reverend Canon Frederick Williams of the Church of the Intercession, addresses the gathering. "Fifteen years of death," says Williams, a slight man with white hair. "I looked at my address book just this morning, and I don't have a page that doesn't have an RIP on at least one line." Williams pauses, gathers himself, and then continues, his voice rising. "Fifteen years of friends, family, and loved ones struck down in the prime of life." A few "amens" filter back from the crowd.

The Black Church's Uneasiness with AIDS

As Williams speaks, Washington surveys the crowd. Some activists are here, but many of these people have come because they feel there's an epidemic brewing and they need to know more about it. He is happy with the size of the turnout, but he wishes that more clergy had shown up. Any effective effort to stop the spread of AIDS in the black population, Washington firmly believes, must include the black church, the one entity that has consistently served as the backbone, conscience, and support network for most of black America. But the black clergy has had a hard time addressing AIDS—with its suggestions of homosexuality, drug use, and immorality. And the Centers for Disease Control, the federal agency in charge of AIDS prevention, has not effectively warned the black community about how the epidemic is changing. Until the African American church comes to terms with AIDS in its community, Washington fears the numbers are going to get worse.

Pastor Washington has reason to be pessimistic. At 51, he has witnessed wholesale losses from his generation. He has seen his fellow clergy—people who have dedicated their lives to empowering and serving the most dispossessed African Americans—condemn and turn their backs on people suffering from AIDS. And he

> *"The [AIDS] virus is now the No. 1 killer of all African Americans between the ages of 25 and 44."*

saw his closest friend, George Edward Canton Jr., die, so ashamed of his disease that for a time he even hid his condition from Washington.

Pastor Washington himself was unaware of the epidemic and its impacts in his own community until one day in 1989 he was approached by Pernessa Seele, administrator of the AIDS Initiative Program at Harlem Hospital. She was concerned about the number of African Americans in the AIDS ward who were being left to die in isolation. She sought to organize Harlem churches to observe a week of prayer for AIDS victims and met with Washington at his church, Memorial Baptist, on 115th Street in Harlem. They talked about AIDS for three hours, and by the end of that time, Washington felt alarmed. "It became very clear to me that no one was dealing with this," he says. "It was like a hurricane was coming and everyone was going through their motions, business as usual." He agreed to help Seele and started listening for stories about the virus. He learned that some members of his own church were infected, some had already lost sons. He realized that if the congregation at Memorial, which was relatively accepting, was keeping quiet about AIDS, then the silence was likely to be even deeper in the larger black community.

With some help from Washington and other clergy, Seele created The Balm in Gilead, an organization designed to educate and engage the black church. Since then, Washington has worked with Seele and many others around the country to raise awareness and federal funding to fight AIDS. Over the past decade, Washington has fought the epidemic through Harlem Congregations for Community Improvement (HCCI), a corporation comprised of 90 New York churches. He founded HCCI in 1985 with a vision to rebuild Harlem, but since 1991, roughly half of its resources

> *"The AIDS epidemic was inflamed by a number of crises that still afflict low-income African Americans."*

have been dedicated to AIDS work. In the year 2000, the staff of HCCI's AIDS division managed to parlay a $2 million budget into low-cost housing for 60 families living with the virus; prevention workshops in churches and community centers; an HIV resource center for the infected that offers the latest information on treatment; and a support network for other New York churches that are trying to develop AIDS ministries.

The work is exhausting, the funds are limited, and often Washington wonders why black church organizations like his—which have the access and the cultural credibility to reach the most at-risk African Americans—still have to battle for adequate government support. And often he contemplates how so many African Americans can remain unaware that they are living in the midst of a deadly health threat. So for Washington, the conclusion of Frederick Williams' address to those who've gathered for the Week of Prayer is especially poignant.

"For the next two minutes, I want you to think of someone you knew, someone close—who has died of AIDS," says Reverend Williams. The room grows quiet. "Then I'm going to ask you to do something. Just stand and name that person you knew who died of this disease, and give thanks for them." He pauses again. "I thank God for Carl."

No one reacts right away. Then a woman rises and speaks the name of a loved one. Two others join her. A few more people tentatively follow. "James," "Morris," and "Patrick" can be made out. Then slowly, as though finding safety in numbers, almost everyone stands and a soft chorus of names fills the room.

Williams waits until there is silence.

"For those of you who are not standing, let me assure you that next year you will be standing."

AIDS and Poverty

Later that evening, Preston Washington is back in his large, cluttered office at Memorial Baptist. His doctorate from Columbia University's Teachers College and framed photographs of his wife and five sons hang on the wall behind him. Washington has a small build, thinning hair, and a Duke Ellington mustache. He has the eloquence and energy of a strong leader, but also a weariness that makes him seem older than his years. "What kind of damn God is this that allows this damn stuff? Babies dying from AIDS?" he asks. "I have to constantly check in with my own faith because this disease threatens every aspect of faith." Over a fried chicken dinner left over from a church meal for the homeless, he explains his sense of the epidemic's impact.

"What AIDS does is exacerbate the problems that already exist in poor, black communities," he says. "We're dealing with an epidemic where every issue related to poverty comes to fruition."

In many ways Washington is right. The AIDS epidemic was inflamed by a number of crises that still afflict low-income African Americans: Heroin addicts infect each other by sharing needles and then bring the virus home to their loved ones; mothers pass HIV on to their babies; inmates contract AIDS in prison. A significant number of young African Americans were infected in the sex-for-drugs trade that exploded with the crack scourge in the late 1980s.

AIDS continues to cross every boundary of age, gender, and sexual orientation in the black population. The CDC estimates that 1 in 50 black men is HIV positive, whereas the infection rate in the general population is roughly 1 in 300. African American women—who are the fastest growing group of AIDS victims in the country—are infected through heterosexual contact an estimated 50 percent of the time.

> *"In black neighborhoods . . . such services as counseling and treatment for sexually transmitted diseases . . . don't exist."*

These numbers have long been rising. As early as 1983, the CDC reported that blacks accounted for 26 percent of the country's infections. And yet, while there has been a massive, 20-year campaign to curtail infection rates among gay white men, the epidemic in the black population has been largely ignored by both the black community and mainstream America.

A Lack of Services

When AIDS struck inner cities, Reaganomics was just getting into full swing, the welfare mother was being held up as a symbol of ridicule, and there was a growing movement afoot to cut "wasteful" federal social programs. African American communities, often fragmented and poor, were already overwhelmed by other crises. They simply did not have the resources, the information, or the political will to mobilize against the slowly unfolding epidemic.

Today, the problem facing health care workers fighting AIDS in black neighborhoods is that, in many instances, such services as counseling and treatment for sexually transmitted diseases and for substance abuse, don't exist. Or where they do, they're not utilized by low-income African Americans, who are often uninsured, don't have primary physicians, and distrust the medical establishment. As a consequence, black Americans frequently fail to get tested, don't seek early medical care, and have a difficult time maintaining the complicated and expensive medication regimens that an HIV infection demands.

Washington has tried to address those problems in Harlem by offering an AIDS program run for and by African Americans. William Lilly, who almost died in 1993 shortly after he was diagnosed with AIDS, credits HCCI with saving his life. When his wife heard about HCCI, Lilly, who was 45 at the time, had wasted from 200 to 98 pounds. "I didn't have the knowledge I have now," recalls Lilly. "All I could see in front of me was dying. I never thought I was going to gain weight again. I gave all my clothes away, and I just stayed in the house."

> *"As more and more African Americans have been personally touched by the epidemic, the silence around AIDS is beginning to break in the black community."*

An HCCI counselor, though, visited him several times and convinced him to attend a support group. In the following months, HCCI set Lilly and his wife up in low-income housing and later employed him as a "peer educator"—one of a group of volunteers that HCCI has trained to administer instant AIDS tests.

Such humane treatment by a black church organization has been rare. Many of the clergy have accepted the conventional wisdom that AIDS is a gay disease. The intense stigma that surrounds homosexuality in the religious community has slowed the church's response to the epidemic. Often, men have told Washington how they've hidden their illness from friends and family to avoid being branded as gay. And repeatedly, he's heard HIV-positive black men describe to him how they've been frozen out of their churches and isolated from their communities. In large cities like New York that kind of ostracism is abating, but even now Washington knows of Harlem mothers who have recently cremated their sons so that their wasted bodies cannot betray their disease at a funeral. He remembers his friend Bruce Wilson. "I watched him deteriorate. I was with him [one night] until four in the morning," says Washington. "I found out he died the day before his funeral. Nobody told nobody about it. Family wanted to keep it a secret."

A Radical Stance

Washington has taken a radical stance in welcoming gay men to Memorial, one of the most established midsize churches in Harlem. He knows that despite being married and having five children, this has sparked rumors about his own sexuality. But that does not bother him. "The tragedy of all this is [that] the healing of AIDS is not just for the person with AIDS," says Washington. "The healing of AIDS is when everything comes out in the open."

Slowly, though, as more and more African Americans have been personally touched by the epidemic, the silence around AIDS is beginning to break in the black community. This year 7,500 congregations participated nationally in the

Week of Prayer. The Congressional Black Caucus pushed the House to appropriate $245.4 million for fiscal year 2000 for AIDS treatment, education, and research in minority communities. Washington hopes that these are signs of a sustainable political mobilization. "This ain't no play stuff," he says grimly. "This is big time. This is warfare."

This year, former Surgeon General Joycelyn Elders spoke about the epidemic to the National Black Ministers Conference at Covenant Church in Harlem. Two days after Washington's breakfast meeting, she was welcomed to the pulpit with loud applause by 40 or so pastors and reverends. "We can't have any more missed opportunities," said Elders, sounding like a preacher herself. "Now we've got to get out during this very important political season and push for the [government funding] that we need." Later, she observed, "The CDC makes it their responsibility to keep data and inform the health practitioners of what's going on, but the places where they're putting the statistics are not often read in the African American community."

The CDC has not focused its AIDS prevention efforts on knocking on church doors or hitting the inner-city streets. Instead, CDC administrators have chosen to devote most of their attention to facilitating the work of government agencies and AIDS organizations. Last year, for instance, the CDC gave around 70 percent of its $656 million AIDS prevention budget to state and city health departments, which, in turn, distributed money to existing health care providers.

The CDC has been operating on the premise that, with some guidance, local governments know best how to fight AIDS locally, and therefore should be given the latitude to spend prevention money as they see fit. As a consequence of this ad hoc approach, the CDC seems to be operating—two decades into the epidemic—without a clear national strategy to fight AIDS.

Recently, a panel of public health experts and activists—convened by the CDC to assess the effectiveness of its HIV and AIDS programs—criticized the agency for failing to track how its AIDS prevention money was actually used and for having insufficient means to assess the effectiveness of its expenditures. The head of CDC's HIV and AIDS unit, Dr. Helene Gayle, says that the agency has heard the criticism and is developing a new strategy for AIDS prevention. But even a new plan may not have much impact, as the agency is still beholden to Congress for funding. And since 1994, the CDC's prevention budget has been raised only 9 percent in real dollars.

> *"In the black community, AIDS is far from being under control."*

Our public health system failed to respond adequately to AIDS when the disease first devastated gay men in the early 1980s. Since then, billions of dollars have been spent on research, services, and prevention. Now, when AIDS is mentioned to people on the street, they often respond with surprise that it's still a crisis. Two of the largest AIDS organizations in the country, AIDS Project Los

Angeles and the Gay Men's Health Crisis in New York, report that private donations for AIDS services and prevention are declining. When AIDS took its first casualties, gay white men organized quickly and won not only the support needed to combat the epidemic but also the country's tolerance and compassion. By the 1990s, virtually every American, having lost loved ones or perhaps seen Tom Hanks in the movie *Philadelphia*, had read, heard, or seen how gay white men had suffered from AIDS. Ironically, one of the obstacles African Americans now face in fighting the epidemic is the very success of the gay community (where infection rates have plateaued), which has given most Americans the false impression that AIDS is now under control.

But in the black community, AIDS is far from being under control. It will be instructive to see how the nation and the government—and African Americans themselves—respond to AIDS now that it is increasingly seen as a black crisis. The funding to fight the epidemic will probably not be wrenched from Congress without the full-fledged support of powerful black organizations like the Urban League, the NAACP, and the Southern Christian Leadership Conference. Pastor Washington believes that what will eventually bring these groups into the fight against AIDS is a growing sentiment in the black community that, "the most important human rights issue facing African Americans today is the equitable distribution of health resources."

One immediate problem in combating the epidemic is that the CDC has not yet fully utilized the black church in the AIDS prevention effort. Elders, for one, believes that's a critical mistake: "The faith-based community reaches a lot of people that the health community doesn't reach," she said recently from her home in Little Rock. "The church is the one organization that African Americans trust. When they're in trouble—grandma's sick, they need to go on welfare—they go to the church."

The closest the CDC has come to working directly with the church has been to establish a "faith initiative." But that agency program is currently limited to one employee and a budget of $2.7 million for the entire country. So, even when faith-based organizations like Pastor Washington's have organized against AIDS, they've been forced to compete with established health care providers for CDC grants. And as a practical matter, most churches don't have the grant-writing teams, the expertise, or—as in HCCI's case—the staff needed to win those awards.

Still, Washington believes that the church holds a key to solving the AIDS crisis in the African American community. It has a role as political advocate—and Washington himself is prepared to go to Capitol Hill the next time the Congressional Black Caucus asks for more AIDS funds. But the church also has a crucial spiritual role to play: to empower people to cope with the issues of poverty, addiction, broken families, and homophobia that have enabled AIDS to spread so rapidly and so deeply. "What we're dealing with now," says Washington, "is the reality of disenfranchisement, the reality of disempowerment, the reality of dehumanization."

When it is time for Pastor Washington to deliver his sermon at Memorial Baptist Church during the AIDS Week of Prayer, he preaches about the biblical story of the nameless man who lay in his own feces and urine just steps from the healing pool of Bethesda [in Maryland]. Washington is in the pulpit and sweat is dripping from his face. A choir of 30 singers is behind him, dressed in white and gold robes. The sanctuary is packed. Washington has just described how the nameless man, after decades of being "disempowered, seemingly unable to help himself," is bathed by Christ in the healing waters. Then Washington compares this nameless man to everyone in the congregation. In the back row, a woman weeps openly. "It's time," Washington says. "It's time. It's time to be healed."

Homosexual Youths Have a Greater Risk of Sexually Transmitted Diseases

by Frank York and Robert H. Knight

About the authors: *Frank York is a former editor in the public policy department of* Focus on the Family. *He is coauthor of* When the Wicked Seize a City, *a history of the gay rights movement in San Francisco. Robert H. Knight is director of cultural studies at the Family Research Council.*

No question about it: both ends of the cultural spectrum acknowledge that self-avowed, practicing homosexual teenagers run grave health risks. Research demonstrates that these adolescents face significantly higher risks of suicide, drug abuse, alcoholism, and sexually transmitted diseases (STDs), particularly acquired immune deficiency syndrome (AIDS).

But *why* homosexual teens face such dangers is widely disputed. Scholars with homosexual sympathies and especially homosexual political activists look to society at large for scapegoats. Never considering the possibility that homosexual behavior itself might be responsible for its documented risks, they cite the bogeyman of "homophobia" and religious intolerance as root causes of the health difficulties of homosexuals, especially as "repressive" social attitudes allegedly lower the self-esteem of those with homosexual tendencies.

In an article published on the Internet, "Problems Faced by Homosexual Youth," lesbian Jenny Gable traces the beginnings of homosexual difficulties to non-acceptance. She writes: "Homosexual youth cannot speak up because of fear and misunderstanding. And when no one speaks up for them, no one stops the pain, many teens cannot handle it and commit suicide." Gable comes down particularly hard on the families of homosexuals:

> Parents, unaware of their children's sexual orientation, often make cutting remarks about homosexual television characters, community members, or the orientation in general. . . . Many times they find hate instead of acceptance,

Excerpted from Frank York and Robert H. Knight, "Homosexual Teens at Risk," *Family Policy*, March/April 1998. Reprinted with permission from Family Research Council.

sometimes to the point of being kicked out of the house at age 14 or 15 when a homophobic parent does find out.

Miss Gable has a point. Many teens who identify themselves as gay face despair and anguish; they become objects of scorn by classmates. Yet many teens experience anguish and difficulty relating to peers for reasons having little to do with sexual orientation. In fact, alienated teens with no homosexual proclivities are targets for gay activists. The activists will embrace these youngsters while offering them an identity by claiming—without credible scientific evidence—that the teens were probably born gay, and then suggest that their alleged homosexuality explains their adjustment problems. For a vulnerable teenager struggling for acceptance, this pitch can sound quite therapeutic.

But what came first, the chicken or the egg—the teenager's social alienation or his homosexuality? One study of Minnesota teens found that as many as 10 percent were uncertain of their sexuality until their later years. Absent pressure from gay recruiters, many of these teens "straighten out" and begin to relate to the opposite sex. But many others are recruited by gay activists while still vulnerable.

Once brought into the homosexual fold, these teens are then plugged into a network of dysfunctional relationships that are, by nature, destructive of self-esteem. They are furthermore introduced to an array of dangerous behaviors, including anal intercourse, sado-masochism, sexual promiscuity, and substance abuse. These pathologies are an integral part of the homosexual lifestyle regardless of the social environment, whether a conservative Bible Belt city like Nashville or a homosexual haven like San Francisco, where the threat of societal disapproval or personal "homophobia" is minimal. Therefore, blaming mainstream heterosexual society for the woes of homosexuals is not simply disingenuous, but overlooks the wealth of research data that demonstrates that homosexual behavior itself is far more hazardous to a teen's health than so-called social homophobia.

Homosexual Health Risks

Sexually transmitted diseases are without a doubt the most serious consequence of homosexual behavior. Practicing homosexuals as a group account for an overwhelmingly disproportionate number of cases of sexually transmitted diseases, including gonorrhea, hepatitis A, hepatitis B, and syphilis. According to the American Medical Association, homosexual youth are twenty-three times more likely to contract sexually transmitted diseases than heterosexuals. In particular, male homosexuals suffer from a unique combination of diseases, including what is termed gay bowel syndrome, caused by parasites exchanged during rectal and oral-anal intercourse, standard sexual practices of homosexual men.

> *"Sexually transmitted diseases are without a doubt the most serious consequence of homosexual behavior."*

Even when using a condom, homosexual men discover that what originally was designed as a birth control device between a man and a woman engaging in natural relations is no guarantee against disease transmission, rectal damage, or even HIV infection. Former Surgeon General C. Everett Koop, who promoted condoms as a part of the government's anti-AIDS strategy, warned against the use of condoms for anal (homosexual) sexual relations. In rather graphic terms, he cut to the heart of the issue:

> The rectum was not made for intercourse. It's at the wrong angle, it's the wrong size, it doesn't have the same kind of tough lining that the vagina does. It has its blood supply directly under the mucosa. Therefore, you would expect a great many more failures of condoms in rectal intercourse than you would in vaginal intercourse, and it's important to know that.

The risk of infection in homosexual relations—even with a condom—is so great that the National Institutes of Health canceled a condom study among young homosexuals in Los Angeles on the grounds that it would be immoral to put the young people at risk. Study director Jeffrey Perlman explained: "In a place like L.A., in the gay community, one would really be talking about delaying the infection rather than preventing it."

> *"Current research . . . reveals a brazen willingness among younger homosexuals to indulge in self-destructive behavior."*

Not only do homosexuals suffer higher risks of sexually transmitted diseases, but once they contract the human immunodeficiency virus (HIV), they tend to encounter a higher "seroconversion" rate to AIDS because of drug use, a behavior that often accompanies homosexual behavior, especially among younger homosexuals (seroconversion is the point at which a person develops antibodies in the blood serum, indicating that HIV infection has occurred). In a study of 337 homosexual men in San Francisco who were initially HIV negative, 39 percent "seroconverted" by the third year. The study revealed that homosexuals who regularly used marijuana, nitrites, cocaine, methamphetamines, hallucinogens, barbiturates, ethyl chloride, opiates, and amphetamines had a higher seroconversion rate to HIV than those who did not. The reasons discovered include:

- The use of stimulants and inhalants is believed to increase sexual drive and may delay ejaculation. Prolonged sexual episodes may result in more damage to rectal membranes, heightening the chances of HIV infection.
- The history of prior drug use is a marker for a general risk-taking disposition that includes the likelihood of dangerous sex practices.
- Drug abuse and sexual behavior may occur in long-standing social relationships. The report states: "Sexual mixing in such networks could result in increased likelihood of HIV seroconversion if unprotected anal intercourse is the network norm and if it occurs in the context of a high background prevalence of HIV infection." Since the proportion of HIV-positive homosexual

men in some urban centers ranges from 30 to 50 percent, the chances of encountering an infected partner in this group are very high.

Risks Among Young Homosexuals

Current research not only demonstrates the health risks of homosexual behavior, but reveals a brazen willingness among younger homosexuals to indulge in self-destructive behavior. A study of young homosexual men by the San Francisco Department of Public Health reported that 33 percent of "high-risk youth" admitted to engaging in unprotected anal intercourse during the previous six months. A Los Angeles study of young homosexual males in 1996 revealed that about half of those between fifteen and twenty-two years of age had engaged in "high-risk, unprotected sex" during the previous six months. As Wesley Ford of the Los Angeles County's HIV epidemiology program lamented in the *Los Angeles Times*, "These are kids with relatively short sexual histories. What will this [group] look like 10 years from now when they have another 10 years of sexual behavior under their belt?"

> *"Young homosexuals are particularly at risk for HIV because many are unaware of their HIV status."*

At the other end of the country, a study of 4,159 Massachusetts high school students discovered a strong correlation of many risk behaviors associated with self-identified "gay, lesbian or bisexual" youth, who comprised 2.5 percent of the sample. The behaviors included suicide, victimization, sexual risk behaviors, and multiple substance abuse such as tobacco, alcohol, marijuana, and cocaine. In addition, gay youths were more likely to report initiating and engaging in multiple risk behaviors at an earlier age than their peers. In another study of 1,086 lesbian and bisexual women, 21 percent of the lesbians reported having high-risk sexual contact, including sex with homosexual men, and 49 percent of bisexual women interviewed reported having high-risk sexual contact. In addition, 9 percent of the lesbian/bisexual women reported a history of intravenous drug abuse.

Young homosexuals are particularly at risk for HIV because many are unaware of their HIV status. Thomas Coates, professor of medicine and director of the Center for AIDS Prevention Studies at University of California at San Francisco, notes that the virus is most infectious in the first months, yet people are least likely to know that they are infected at that point because the antibodies that indicate HIV remain undetected, on average, for six months. Coates believes that condom-based prevention campaigns have worked for men more than thirty years of age but not for younger gay men.

Even in the face of public service and education campaigns that warn about the dangers of unprotected sex and HIV infection, young homosexuals continue to engage in behaviors that will most certainly lead to premature mortality. A cover story in the *Los Angeles Times* magazine featured a number of young men who were HIV positive (or would eventually become so) who risk death in pursuit of the perfect orgasm.

One man featured named Gabe had begun engaging in homosexual relations when he was sixteen and well aware of the dangers of HIV infection. Yet, according to the magazine feature, "he voluntarily and repeatedly engaged in unprotected sex with men whose chances of having HIV could be conservatively estimated at

> *"Another factor that makes homosexual conduct . . . so risky is the reluctance of HIV-infected homosexual men to inform sexual partners of their infection."*

one in three." Another young man, Alex, ran away from home at the age of eleven because he could not stand his mother and her series of boyfriends. He ended up on the streets of Hollywood, where an older man named Wayne befriended him in front of a gay and lesbian center. Wayne invited the boy to live with him, but he also gave him an unexpected surprise: the AIDS virus. By age fifteen, Alex was infected. When interviewed three years later, he remarked: "Even before Wayne, I never practiced safe sex, . . . I didn't know condoms existed. I mean, I knew about condoms. I just didn't know what they were for. And even if I had known, it wouldn't have made any difference. I just thought, 'I'm so cute, and I'm so good in bed, nothing will happen to me.'"

Many Remain Quiet About Their HIV Status

Another factor that makes homosexual conduct and behavior so risky is the reluctance of HIV-infected homosexual men to inform sexual partners of their infection, as documented by a Brown University study. The study revealed that while three-quarters of HIV-infected women told their sexual partners they have HIV, only one-half of HIV-infected men did so. "Even after years of education, too many HIV carriers are willing to spread the misery than risk rejection," the study concluded, warning: "Would-be lovers beware."

Further intensifying these documented risks, a new group of young homosexual radicals called Sex Panic is telling the "safe-sex" crusaders to get lost. They insist that unprotected sex is something worth dying for. Anal sex without condoms, according to Sex Panic, makes a needed statement of sexual freedom and homosexual identity, a statement that for some homosexuals is worth more than their lives or the lives of their partners. This approach has critics including other homosexual activists who seek to understand what drives such blatant recklessness. Eric Rofes, former director of an AIDS support group, the Shanti Project, claims that homosexuals take such risks because homosexual identity is so wrapped up with anal intercourse; a condom, apparently, weakens that identity. He says, "Sex acts are a major part of what constitutes your identity . . . anal sex was seen as an expendable act. . . . It gives meaning to who you are, as a gay man."

Other critics are less understanding. David Dalton, a homosexual computer systems engineer for the *San Francisco Examiner*, editorialized against Sex Panic in the newspaper for whom he works:

> The gay community in San Francisco is large, secure, mature, and diverse. Many of us—maybe most of us—are in the mainstream because that's where we want to be. It's all right to stand up to the brats in Sex Panic and say in a loud, firm voice: Stop claiming to speak for all of us.

> And if you insist on rebelling (I'm sure you will), then please consider rebelling against Sex Panic, the people who are telling you that a sex act—any sex act—is worth more than your life.

Dalton's advice may be commendable, yet he fails to consider that anal sex is dangerous in *any* form, with or without a condom. The difference is like smoking cigarettes with or without a filter; the practice is simply hazardous to one's health. Homosexuals engaging in promiscuous sex without condoms can be nearly 100 percent certain they will eventually become infected. The odds of becoming infected are somewhat less with a condom, but upon infection, premature death is still the result. Biochemist and molecular biologist David Collart writes: "Studies show the rate of HIV infection associated with condom use ranges from 13 percent to 27 percent. In a study where heterosexual couples used condoms, 17 percent of partners of AIDS patients became infected within 18 months." A condom may extend the time before infection occurs, but it is only a delay.

The Best Interests of "the Children"

One would think the clear health risks involved in homosexual behavior would discourage its social acceptance, yet just the opposite seems to be the case as "gay affirming" campaigns have expanded across the country in the past decade, including initiatives to counter "homophobia" among school children. The videotape, *It's Elementary*, a pro-homosexual documentary, has been shown to public elementary school teachers. Children's books such as *Heather Has Two Mommies* and *Daddy's Roommate* have been placed on the shelves of some public and school libraries with little opposition. A book for pre-teens that carries an Ann Landers endorsement, *It's Perfectly Normal*, presents homosexuality as a positive, matter-of-fact behavior. These efforts have more or less the blessing of President Bill Clinton, who at a 1997 White House press conference on hate crimes, endorsed the idea that elementary school children need to be taught tolerance toward homosexuality.

> *"Homosexuals engaging in promiscuous sex without condoms can be nearly 100 percent certain they will eventually become infected [with HIV]."*

According to Joseph Nicolosi, a licensed psychologist who specializes in gender identity research, such efforts to normalize homosexuality are clearly not in the best interests of "the children," as the Clintons are fond of saying. Founder of the National Association for the Research and Therapy of Homosexuals, Nicolosi says that boys with an unmet need for masculine affirmation are vulnerable to homosexual seduction. When a boy's otherwise healthy drive to gain masculine identity becomes sexualized, homosexuality can result first as an experiment and later as a habitual way of life, especially if parents, teachers, and other role models view homosexuality as harmless. . . .

Protecting the Young from Gay Bondage

How to protect vulnerable teens from becoming trapped in an addictive sexual behavior may not be as easy, given today's cultural climate. But there is hope. At one level, parents, teachers, social workers, and clergy need to challenge the nonsense set forth by homosexual activists that homosexuality is simply an alternative lifestyle or a harmless diversion. They need to view homosexuality in a more realistic fashion, seeing it for what it really is: a life-controlling addiction like smoking or drug abuse.

At the institutional level, school board members and administrators, as well as college and university officials, need to say no to gay-affirming counseling programs, which are geared to encourage, not discourage, homosexuality among young people. Librarians will need to think about the value of keeping books like *Heather Has Two Mommies* or *Daddy's Roommate* in general circulation. If teens are seduced into associations with older homosexuals who engage in high risk behaviors, they will invariably be at risk for this addictive sexual behavior, as well as HIV infection.

Most important, parents need to model healthy heterosexual love and monogamous marriage to their adolescent children. Children receive plenty of negative input from the media, peers, and even from some teachers. But nothing communicates better to struggling adolescents than loving acceptance by parents who spend time with their children, listen, and create a warm and nurturing home as a refuge from the outside world. In that nonthreatening context, parents can facilitate meaningful discussions about sex and gender issues with teenagers, pointing out the dangers of pre-marital sex, including homosexual conduct. Even in the best of homes, some children will struggle with sexual identity issues, but sensitive parents can challenge them to express their manhood or womanhood in responsible ways. Once an adolescent senses that his parents understand his situation and is assured that his parents are committed to helping him overcome any gender identity confusion, many potential crises can be averted. Parents then can be confident that members of the next generation will move into mature adulthood, expressing their sexuality in a responsible, heterosexual fashion—that is, in marriage as husbands and wives.

AIDS Is Increasingly Afflicting Latinos

by Ann Louise Bardach

About the author: *Ann Louise Bardach is a contributing editor of* Vanity Fair.

Freddie Rodriguez is discouraged. He has just come from his afternoon's activity of trying to stop men from having unprotected sex in Miami's Alice Wainwright Park, a popular gay cruising spot. Rodriguez, 29, is a slim, handsome Cuban-American with a pale, worried face who works for Health Crisis Network. "I take a bag of condoms to the park with me and I try talking to people before they duck in the bushes and have sex," he explains. "I tell them how dangerous it is. Sometimes I beg them to use a condom. Sometimes they listen to me. Today, no one was interested." Most of the men, he says, are Latinos and range in age from 16 to 60. Many are married and would never describe themselves as gay. "Discrimination is not really the issue here. Most Latinos do not identify themselves as gay, so they're not discriminated against," he says, his voice drifting off. "Ours is a culture of denial."

To understand why the second wave of AIDS is hitting Latinos particularly hard, one would do well to start in Miami. Once a mecca for retirees, South Beach today is a frenzy of dance and sex clubs, for hetero- and homosexual alike. "We have the highest rate of heterosexual transmission in the country, the second-highest number of babies born with AIDS and we are number one nationwide for teen HIV cases," says Randi Jenson, reeling off a litany that clearly exhausts him. Jenson supervises the Miami Beach HIV/AIDS Project and sits on the board of the Gay, Lesbian and Bisexual Community Center. "And we have the highest rate of bisexuality in the country." When I ask how he knows this, he says, "Trust me on this one, we know. . . . The numbers to watch for in the future will be Hispanic women—the wives and girlfriends."

Hispanics and AIDS

Already, AIDS is the leading cause of death in Miami and Fort Lauderdale for women ages 25 to 44, four times greater than the national average. According to the Centers for Disease Control and Prevention (CDC), AIDS cases among Hispanics have been steadily rising. But any foray into the Latino subculture shows that the numbers do not tell the whole story, and may not even tell half. CDC literature notes that "it is believed that AIDS-related cases and deaths for Latinos are understated by at least 30 percent. Many Hispanics do not and cannot access HIV testing and health care." Abetted by widespread shame about homosexuality, a fear of governmental and medical institutions (particularly among undocumented immigrants) and cultural denial as deep as Havana Harbor, AIDS is moving silently and insistently through Hispanic America. It is the stealth virus.

"No one knows how many Latino HIV cases are out there," Damian Pardo, an affable Cuban-American, who is president of the board of Health Crisis Network, tells me over lunch in Coral Gables. "All we know is that the numbers are not accurate—that the actual cases are far higher. Everyone in the community lies about HIV." Everyone, according to Pardo, means the families, the lovers, the priests, the doctors and the patients. "The Hispanic community in South Florida is far more affluent than blacks. More often than not, people see their own family doctor who simply signs a falsified death certificate. It's a conspiracy of silence and everyone is complicitous."

Freddie Rodriguez—smart, affluent, urbane—didn't learn that Luis, his Nicaraguan lover, was HIV-positive until it was too late to do anything about it. "He was my first boyfriend. He would get sick at times but he refused to take a blood test. He said that it was impossible for him to be HIV-positive. I believed him. One day, he disappeared. Didn't come home, didn't go to work—just disappeared." Frantic, Rodriguez called the police and started phoning hospitals. Finally, Luis turned up at Jackson Memorial Hospital. He had been discovered unconscious and rushed to intensive care. When Rodriguez arrived at the hospital, he learned that his lover was in the AIDS wing. Even then, Luis insisted it was a mistake. Two weeks later, he was dead. "I had to tell Luis's family that he was gay," Rodriguez says, "that I was his boyfriend and that he had died of AIDS. They knew nothing. He lived a completely secret life."

Although Rodriguez was enraged by his lover's cowardice, he understood his dilemma all too well. He remembered how hard it was to tell his own family. "When I was 22, I finally told my parents that I was gay. My mother screamed and ran out of the room. My father raised his hands in front of his eyes and told me, 'Freddie do you see what's in front of me? It's a big, white cloud. I do not hear anything, see anything and I cannot remember anything because it is all in this big white cloud.' And then he left the room." One of Rodriguez's later boyfriends, this one Peruvian, was also HIV-positive, but far more duplicitous. "He flat out lied

> *"'Most Latinos do not identify themselves as gay, so they're not discriminated against. . . . Ours is a culture of denial.'"*

to me when I asked him. He knew, but he only told me after we broke up, after we had unsafe sex," says Rodriguez, who remains HIV-negative. "Part of the machismo ethic," Rodriguez explains, "is not wearing a condom."

Latino Culture and the Spread of AIDS

Miami's Body Positive, which provides psychological and non-clinical services to AIDS patients, is housed in a pink concrete bubble off Miami's Biscayne Boulevard. The building and much of its funding are provided by founder Doris Feinberg, who lost both her sons to AIDS during the late 1980s. The gay Cuban-American star of MTV's *The Real World*, Pedro Zamora, worked here for the last five years of his life and started its P.O.P. program—Peer Outreach for Persons Who Are Positive. Ernie Lopez, a 26-year-old Nicaraguan who has been Body Positive's director for the last five years, estimates that 40 percent of the center's clients are Latino, in a Miami population that is 70 percent Hispanic. On the day I visit, I see mostly black men at the facility. Lopez warns me not to be fooled. "The Latino numbers are as high as the blacks, but they are not registered," he says. "Latinos want anonymity. They come in very late—when they are desperate and their disease is very progressed. Often it's too late to help them."

"Soy completo," is what they often say in Cuba, meaning, "I'm a total human being." It is the preferred euphemism for bisexuality and in the machista politics of Latino culture, bisexuality is a huge step up from being gay. It is this cultural construct that prevents many Latin men from acknowledging that they could be vulnerable to HIV, because it is this cultural construct that tells them they are not gay. Why worry about AIDS if only gay men get AIDS? "To be bisexual is a code," says Ernesto Pujol, a pioneer in Latino AIDS education. "It means, 'I sleep with men but I still have power.' I think there is a legitimate group of bisexuals, but for many bisexuality is a codified and covered homosexuality." Self-definitions can get even more complex. "I'm not gay," a well-known intellectual told me in Havana last year. "How could I be gay? My boyfriend is married and has a family."

> *"'According to the Centers for Disease Control and Prevention (CDC), AIDS cases among Hispanics have been steadily rising.'"*

Latinos and Homosexuality

Without putting too fine a point on it, what defines a gay man in some segments of the Latino world is whether he's on the top or the bottom during intercourse. "The salient property of the maricon," my Cuban friend adds, "is his passivity. If you're a 'top,'—el bugaron—you're not a faggot." Moreover, there are also many heterosexual Latino men who do not regard sex with another man as a homosexual act. "A lot of heterosexual Latinos—say, after a few drinks—will fuck a transvestite as a surrogate woman," says Pujol, "and that is culturally acceptable—absolutely acceptable." Hence the potential for HIV transmission is far greater than in the mainstream Anglo world.

According to Pujol, "only Latinos in the States are interested in other gay men. They have borrowed the American liberated gay model. In Latin America, the hunt is for 'straight' men. Look at the transvestites on Cristina's (the Spanish-language equivalent of "Oprah") talk show. Their boyfriends are always some macho hunk from the bodega." Chino, a Cuban gay now living in Montreal, typifies the cultural divide.

> *"The Latino [AIDS] numbers are as high as the blacks."*

"I don't understand it here," he says scornfully. "It's like girls going out with girls."

"If you come out," says Jorge B., a Cuban artist in Miami Beach, "you lost your sex appeal to 'straight' men" (straight in this context meaning married men who have sex with other men). The Hispanic preference for "straight men" is so popular that bathhouses such as Club Bodycenter in Coral Gables are said to cater to a clientele of older married men who often pick up young lovers after work before joining their families for dinner. Some men will not risk going to a gay bar, says Freddie Rodriguez. "They go to public restrooms where they can't be identified." While many gay Hispanics do eventually "come out," they do so at a huge price—a shattering loss of esteem within their family and community. "The priest who did Mass at my grandfather's funeral denied communion to me and my brother," recalls Pardo. "He knew from my mother's confession that we were gay."

Latino attitudes here are, of course, largely imported, their cultural fingerprints lifted straight out of Havana, Lima or Guatemala City. Consider Chiapas, Mexico, where gay men were routinely arrested throughout the 1980s; many of their bodies were later found dumped in a mass grave. Or Ecuador, where it is against the law to be a homosexual, and effeminate behavior or dress can be grounds for arrest. Or Peru, where the Shining Path has targeted gays for assassination. Or Colombia, where death squads do the same, characteristically mutilating their victims' genitals.

While Latino hostility to homosexuals in the United States tends to be less dramatic, it can also be virulent, particularly when cradled in reactionary politics. In Miami, right-wing Spanish-language stations daily blast their enemies as "communists, traitors and Castro puppets." But the epithet reserved for the most despised is "homosexual" or "maricon." When Nelson Mandela visited Miami in 1990, he was denounced daily as a "marijuanero maricon"—a pot-smoking faggot—for having supported Fidel Castro.

Closeted Latinos Hinder Prevention Efforts

On the other side of the country, AIDS Project Los Angeles is the second-largest health provider for AIDS patients in the United States (after Gay Men's

Health Crisis in New York). It's a sparkling facility with a food bank, a dental program and all manner of support services. Housed in the David Geffen Building at the corner of Fountain and Vine, it is well-provided for by a generous Hollywood community. Currently, AIDS Project Los Angeles attends to the needs of more than 4,500 clients, 60 percent of whom are gay men. Roughly one-fourth of the total are Latinos, and the majority of those are Mexican. Thirty-two-year-old Troy Fernandez is one of the project's senior aides on public policy. Born in Yonkers and of Puerto Rican descent, Fernandez is a caramel-colored black man with long dreadlocks streaming down his back. Dressed in crisp white jeans, he's as slim and elegant as a fountain pen. He's also HIV-positive—part of the second wave.

Although Fernandez "did the downtown dance scene and Fire Island," in his 20s, he didn't go to the bathhouses, and he was never on the front line of the party scene. Even when the political equation of the gay revolution—"the more promiscuous, the more liberated"—still had currency, Fernandez was warier than his peers. By 1981, friends of his had started to die of the mysterious illness then known as the gay plague. Fernandez got himself checked out as soon as HIV testing became available, and came up negative year after year while he continued to practice safe sex. Then he moved to Los Angeles and met Rodrigo.

Rodrigo was a well-educated Mexican-American, a high-level insurance executive, a Republican conservative and "completely closeted." Among Rodrigo's tightly knit family, only one of his brothers—also gay—knew his secret. When Fernandez asked his partner if he was HIV-positive, he said no. He'd never been tested, but he knew he wasn't. He also insisted he was monogamous. "It's all about what risks you are willing to take," says Fernandez slowly. "I understand why people stop practicing safe sex. One is always renegotiating the risk factors at some level. You see, you want to believe that your lover is telling you the truth."

In 1990, Rodrigo got sick. By then Fernandez had become suspicious, and pressed his partner to be tested. "I told him he had to do it for my sake," he says, "if nothing else." When Rodrigo learned he was positive "it was a double whammy," says Fernandez. "He had to admit that he was sick and dying and worse—he had to admit that he was gay." Within the year, Fernandez learned that he, too, had the virus. Remembering, he lets loose a long sigh. "I don't have an answer for why I took a chance. I knew better, but it only takes one time." Fernandez surmises on the basis of personal anecdotal experience that as many as "90 percent [of gay] Latinos are closeted. Many may have self-identified but tell no one else." He bases his estimate on the number of married men who come into AIDS Project Los Angeles. "They always say they need the information for their brother or brother-in-law."

Total Denial

Rarely visible in the statistics are the wives and girlfriends of these men—the group that experts predict will soar to the top of the AIDS charts. Currently, blacks and Latinas make up 77 percent of all AIDS cases among women; the number of Latina cases is seven times higher than that of Anglo women. Researchers have long known that the "receptive partner," is at greater risk of contracting not only HIV but all sexually transmitted diseases. For reasons generally unknown, women tend to get sicker sooner and die faster. Moreover, for many Latinas striving to be good Catholic wives in a culture where church and family are the co-pillars of the community, contracting HIV is an unfathomable betrayal and an irredeemable disgrace.

> *"Currently, blacks and Latinas make up 77 percent of all AIDS cases among women; the number of Latina cases is seven times higher than that of Anglo women."*

Ernesto Pujol remembers a Salvadoran housewife in her mid-50s, then living in Brooklyn. "She had just tested positive. She was crying. She was so bitter—so angry at her husband and the waste of her life. She had bought the whole Latina martyrdom of being the faithful wife." The husband was a drunk who had battered her, belittled her, and who would finally kill her. Still, she maintained that her husband had been infected by female prostitutes—and never looked at the evidence that he had had sex with men. "None of the women I worked with ever admitted that their spouses were gay or bisexual," says Pujol. "They would say, 'He drinks, you know.' They would rather blame prostitutes than consider the culturally unacceptable possibility of other men."

Wanda Santiago, 36, has lived much of her life as a pariah. A Puerto Rican lesbian, born and raised in Brooklyn, Santiago learned in 1989 that she was HIV-positive. At 13, she started doing drugs when her family moved to a rough neighborhood in Williamsburg. At 16, she was pregnant and married and drinking. After three years, her husband left. "I knew I was gay since I was 8," she says, "but I thought getting married would cure me." In 1978, Santiago came out and turned the care of her young son over to her mother.

Santiago suspects she contracted HIV during her romance with an Ecuadoran woman who was stationed with the Navy in Virginia. "I was crazy about her," says Santiago, who lived with the woman for three years. "Every now and then, she would bring a man to our bed," says Santiago. "It could have been one of them, or maybe I got it from a needle." A few years after her relationship hit the skids, Santiago sobered up for good, but by then she was feeling tired all the time. "For a week after I tested positive, I refused to believe it," she says. "Total denial."

Until 1991, Santiago worked for the Health & Rehabilitation Service screening Latinas with sexually transmitted diseases for HIV. "A lot of them refused to be tested," she says. "If they did test positive, they wouldn't believe it. The fear overwhelmed them. They would say, 'Don't talk about it,' 'I don't have it' and 'Don't tell my husband.' Many were in denial about their husbands screwing around. They thought they would get blamed for getting the disease. It's much worse in Hispanic culture than it is for whites or blacks because Hispanics won't even talk about it. A lot of the women were afraid to use condoms because they would get beat up by their husbands. See, if you're infected by a man, you're a whore. If you're infected by drugs, then you deserve it. But it's OK for a man to have HIV because it's OK for a man to whore around."

"They Didn't Have AIDS"

Mary Lou Duran has been working with the community in East Los Angeles for twenty-one years, the last three and a half of them as a case manager for the HIV patients at Altamed Services. Her clients are women: primarily Mexican-American or Central American refugees, both legal and undocumented, ranging in age from 17 to 56, and including "several grandmothers." A few of the older women may have gotten the virus from blood transfusions during surgery in Mexico, before the availability of HIV testing. But the overwhelming majority were infected by spouses or lovers. "One woman, from Guatemala, died in October," Duran says. "She had a very aggressive virus and died in less than three and a half years. She got it from a boyfriend and left a child behind. I feel the majority of the women I see are innocent victims—wives and girlfriends who have no idea what is going on." Duran then relates a more personal experience: "In my own family, there have been three deaths—three nephews who were gay. But my family says, 'No one has died of AIDS.' They call it cancer. We can't comfort each other because we can't discuss it. 'They weren't gay,' they say, and 'They didn't have AIDS.'"

By coincidence, one of Duran's ailing nephews ran into her at a clinic where she was working. "He was shocked to see me," she remembers. "He was sick—very progressed by the time he came in for help." They chatted briefly, awkwardly. It was her only personal contact with the tragedy in her family. "I have always been a community worker and my family has come to me when they have a need of sorts, but never while I do this work. They have never asked for my help. They have no interest or curiosity in my work. They never ask any questions. Nothing is ever said. The entire community is in denial. They just don't believe it is happening. They think that AIDS is about gay white males."

> *"Many [Latinas] were in denial about their husbands screwing around."*

Intervention

When not manning the AIDS project, Troy Fernandez makes the rounds of Hollywood bathhouses, doing what amounts to "interventions"—foisting condoms on men before they have sex. "The culture of the bathhouses has changed," he says, his voice brightening. "Some people sit around and talk.

Sure, it's still mainly sex but there's some talk." Fernandez doesn't believe closing the bathhouses serves any purpose. "If you close the Hollywood Spa or the Compound, people will simply go to Plummer Park or the restroom at the Beverly Center. My friends in New York say the bathrooms at Juilliard are very busy these days. Face it, we are not going to stop people from having sex."

What then are the prospects of halting the second wave? Fernandez is initially speechless, and it takes a few minutes for him to get pumped up again. "We should get real that what we're doing is not working." He sings the praises of another program he's involved in—Saber es Poder (Knowledge is Power), which enables him and others to go into heavily Hispanic schools and talk to kids in grades seven through twelve. "But I can't say 'dick' to a kid in a school program without losing funding," he complains. "The truth is, Joycelyn Elders was right. We have to start talking to kids when they're young, not when it's too late or the second wave will keep rolling along and then the third wave and then the fourth wave."

As for Ernesto Pujol, he says he will never forget Carla, a soft-spoken, graceful Puerto Rican he met during his days running the Brooklyn AIDS unit of New York's Crisis Intervention Services. Happily married to a Brazilian man, Carla was at work on her doctorate. "The entire family got sick about the same time," says Pujol. "Her husband, she and their 2-year-old daughter. He died first, then the baby. I remember the day in the hospital that she told her family that she had AIDS and of course they became hysterical. It was very sad. She was a devout Catholic and AIDS caused her a great crisis of faith—like a slap in the face. As a couple, they had everything going for them—white upper-middle-class Latinos who could pass, educated and charming. Her husband had told her that he got it from an old girlfriend who was an addict but I suspected that he had had prior bisexual behavior. She chose to believe what her husband told her and I wasn't about to take that away from her. He was a very terrific, wonderful guy who was also working on his doctorate. But he was haunted by his past—and HIV is a past that won't ever let go of you."

Drug Users and Their Partners Are at Risk of Contracting Sexually Transmitted Diseases

by the National Institute on Drug Abuse

About the author: *The National Institute on Drug Abuse (NIDA), is part of the National Institutes of Health (NIH), the principal biomedical and behavioral research agency of the U.S. government. NIH is a component of the U.S. Department of Health and Human Services.*

There is little doubt today about the connection between drug use and HIV infection, which leads to AIDS. What might be less well appreciated, but just as true, is the strong connection between drug use and other infectious diseases, particularly hepatitis C and tuberculosis. Drug use is now the major risk factor identified in new cases of AIDS, hepatitis C, and tuberculosis in the United States, and a growing number of cases of these infectious diseases are now reported among the partners of intravenous drug users. In addition, the majority of HIV-infected newborns have mothers who were infected through their own drug use or through sexual activity with a drug user.

The urgency of the problem comes from statistics such as these: One study of street-recruited intravenous drug users and crack cocaine smokers found that among the intravenous drug users, HIV seroprevalence was 12.7 percent, and among crack smokers, HIV seroprevalence was 7.5 percent. Therefore, the National Institute on Drug Abuse's (NIDA) top priorities in dealing with this issue continue to be to understand the behaviors that put drug users at risk for contracting HIV and other infectious diseases, expand outreach to educate populations at risk about the relationship between drug use and AIDS as well as other infectious diseases, and fund research on drug use behaviors that lead to the transmission of HIV and other infectious diseases.

Excerpted from the National Institute on Drug Abuse, "Drug Abuse and Addiction Research: The Sixth Triennial Report to Congress," 2000, available at www.nida.nih.gov/sTRC/role3.html.

Because of the magnitude of this problem, NIDA has established a Center for AIDS and Other Medical Consequences of Drug Abuse. This office is spearheading the Institute's efforts to expand outreach to educate populations at risk about the relationship between drug use and serious infectious diseases. Research has repeatedly shown that even small amounts of education and counseling can help drug users modify those behaviors that put them at risk for acquiring and transmitting HIV, hepatitis, or tuberculosis, even without total abstinence.

With the establishment of this Center, NIDA has the unique opportunity to assess both short- and long-term consequences associated with drug use, many of which are not well understood. In addition to studying infectious diseases, the Center will also assess other health consequences associated with continued exposure to various illicit drugs, such as the respiratory and pulmonary effects of long-term marijuana smoking. . . .

Characterizing HIV Risk Behaviors

One of the most important areas of research involves understanding the behaviors that drug users engage in that put them at risk for contracting life-threatening diseases. A group of investigators in Seattle, where methamphetamine abuse is a growing problem, have characterized drug use and sexual risk behaviors, social and ecological contexts, and service needs of men who use drugs and have sex with men. Three methods were used for this research: unobtrusive observations, focus group interviews, and individual interviews. Nearly all the men interviewed were HIV positive or had an AIDS diagnosis, and almost all identified themselves as gay or bisexual. A number of common themes emerged from the interviews: Almost all those interviewed injected methamphetamine and used other drugs (e.g., cocaine, MDMA, alcohol, marijuana, heroin); almost all described an intense association between methamphetamine use and sex; and some of the men said they had moved to Seattle specifically because it had a reputation as "the hot spot" for men who use drugs and have sex with men. Although some respondents had completed treatment and remained abstinent from methamphetamine for a period of time, most had also relapsed, explaining that they were unable to enjoy sex without methamphetamine. Abstaining from methamphetamine use was perceived as equivalent to abstaining from sex and therefore made treatment entry and compliance options of last resort. The researchers learned that methamphetamine was sometimes used by respondents to manage the depression they felt from being HIV positive or having AIDS. At the same time, they learned that needle-sharing and unprotected sex were common among the men who reported being HIV seropositive or having AIDS, either because they assumed their inject-

"There is little doubt today about the connection between drug use and HIV infection."

ing drug and sexual partners were also HIV positive or because they would become so intoxicated that they would forget that they were HIV positive.

Another group of researchers in Dayton, Ohio, conducted a study to determine factors that affect the self-reported use of condoms among heterosexual injection drug users and crack cocaine smokers. More than 70 percent of the participants reported that they frequently used drugs when having sex. Persons who were high when they had sex were significantly less likely to use condoms than persons who were not high, but those whose partners got high when having sex were more likely to report condom use. Individuals said that they were less likely to use condoms when they had sex with a main partner. Those who believed it was important to use condoms were more likely to use them, whereas persons who believed condoms reduced sexual pleasure were significantly less likely to use them. A key result of this research is that drug users frequently use substances before and during sex, presenting a significant impediment to employing safer sex techniques that rely on condoms. This study shows that it is also critical that sexual risk-reduction interventions targeting heterosexual users of injection drugs or crack address the widespread practice of simultaneous use of psychoactive drugs. Until such dually focused interventions are in place, access to drug use treatment will continue to play a critical role in preventing the spread of HIV and other sexually transmitted diseases in this population. . . .

> *"Persons who were high when they had sex were significantly less likely to use condoms than persons who were not high."*

Drug Use and Other Infectious Diseases

In addition to its role in the spread of AIDS, illicit drug injection is becoming an increasingly more important niche for the transmission of other diseases, such as tuberculosis, that have significant interactions with HIV-related immunosuppression. For many emerging and re-emerging infectious diseases, protecting the health of the community as a whole will depend on protecting the health of intravenous drug users. Therefore, it is important to learn more about the incidence of infectious diseases in the population of those who abuse drugs.

One study of intravenous drug users found that this population is an important reservoir for hepatitis A infection. The data indicated that intravenous drug users are at increased risk for hepatitis A infection but that factors related to low socioeconomic status, such as poor hygiene or overcrowding, contribute more to the occurrence of hepatitis A infection than does injection drug use. The findings from this study indicate the need for hepatitis A vaccination of intravenous drug users and persons at risk for injection drug use.

Another investigation examined the prevalence and correlates of four blood-borne viral infections among illicit drug users with up to 6 years of injecting history, and data were analyzed for hepatitis C, hepatitis B, and HIV. Overall seroprevalence of hepatitis C, hepatitis B, and HIV was 76.9 percent, 65.7 percent, and 20.5 percent, respectively, for those injecting for up to 6 years. Among those injecting for 1 year or less, rates were 64.7 percent for hepatitis C, 49.8 percent for hepatitis B, and 13.9 percent for HIV. The high rates of viral infections among even short-term injectors emphasize the need to target both parenteral and sexual risk-reduction interventions early.

"One study of intravenous drug users found that this population is an important reservoir for hepatitis A infection."

The danger of these viral infections does not stop with the infected individual. A study from the Women and Infant Transmission Study demonstrated that maternal infection with hepatitis C virus (HCV) is associated with increased HIV maternal-infant transmission. Among women infected with HIV either heterosexually or through injection drug use, 33 percent were found to be infected with hepatitis C, and HIV transmission to infants occurred in 26 percent of the HIV/hepatitis C-infected mothers versus 16 percent of mothers not infected with hepatitis C virus. These data suggest that maternal HCV infection either enhances HIV transmission to the fetus directly or is a marker for another cofactor, such as maternal drug use. Further study is needed to confirm the findings of this study and to determine whether the association represents a biologic effect of hepatitis C infection or is due to a confounding interaction with drug use or other factors.

Chapter 3

How Can Sexually Transmitted Diseases Be Prevented?

Chapter Preface

The human immunodeficiency virus (HIV), widely acknowledged to be the cause of AIDS, is most commonly spread through the sharing of contaminated needles by intravenous drug users, semen during sexual intercourse, and from mother to child during pregnancy or delivery. Although the virus is often transmitted during homosexual sex between men, an increasing number of women are contracting HIV by means of heterosexual intercourse. In 1996, 40 percent of the women who were diagnosed with HIV were infected through heterosexual intercourse.

AIDS activists and researchers advocate the use of condoms as a prevention method, but condoms are not an option for many women whose male partners refuse to use them. However, women may soon have a new alternative to condoms—microbicides, chemical compounds that are inserted into the woman's vagina in the form of a gel or suppository. Microbicides have killed HIV, gonorrhea, chlamydia, herpes, and other sexually transmitted diseases in test tubes. One study found that the microbicide nonoxynol-9 was highly effective in preventing HIV transmission in women who used the agent every other day. Proponents of microbicides assert that the agents are the only prevention method that leaves the woman completely in control of protecting herself from HIV and other sexually transmitted diseases.

Microbicides do have their critics, however. Some contend that the availability of microbicides will encourage women to stop using condoms and other proven HIV prevention methods. Others cite a study of prostitutes who used twice the recommended dosage of nonoxynol-9; the high dosages apparently caused ulcerations in the vagina that could increase the likelihood of HIV infection.

Scientists are studying other types of microbicides as well, such as temperature-sensitive gels and compounds that prevent viral cells from attaching to vaginal cells. Most researchers agree that despite the microbicides' presumed efficacy against HIV transmission, other preventive measures should be used along with the microbicides to strengthen a woman's total protection. Some of these other methods for preventing HIV transmission are examined by the authors in the following chapter.

Preventing HIV Infection

by Thomas J. Coates and Chris Collins

About the authors: *Thomas J. Coates is the director of the AIDS Research In-stitute at the University of California, San Francisco. Chris Collins is an appro-priations associate for Congresswoman Nancy Pelosi of San Francisco.*

With a vaccine still years away, the only broadly applicable way to prevent new HIV infections is to change behaviors that enable transmission of those infections—especially behaviors relating to sex and drug injection.

Because most people simply will not choose celibacy, realistic public health workers have focused on encouraging adoption of safer sexual practices, no-tably condom use. That people can be persuaded to employ safer sex is well il-lustrated by the experience of San Francisco's gay community in the 1980s. Perhaps 8,000 individuals became infected with HIV in both 1982 and 1983. That figure declined to 1,000 a decade later and is now estimated at less than 400 a year. The primary reason for this decline was a precipitous decrease in unprotected anal intercourse as a result of education about safer sex practices.

Targeted education aimed at a particular at-risk community is a prime way to persuade people to engage in preventive practices. In San Francisco, informa-tion about HIV transmission and safer sex was made available in the media and at centers of gay society, such as churches, gay organizations and clubs. Pro-grams aimed at the commercial sex industry have greatly lowered the risks of HIV transmission for both worker and client. In Thailand the Ministry of Public Health has attempted to inspire 100 percent condom use in brothels. It provides condoms and advocates safer sex practices through the media. From 1991 to 1995 the number of men who wore condoms when with prostitutes at brothels rose from 61 to 92.5 percent. HIV infection rates among Thai army conscripts fell from 12.5 percent in 1993 to 6.7 percent in 1995 because condom use was effective and also in part because fewer men employed prostitutes.

Testing and follow-up counseling reduce risk behaviors among both infected and uninfected individuals, as has been documented in a large study in three develop-ing countries. A number of research efforts involving "discordant" heterosexual couples—where only one partner is HIV positive—have shown that counseling following a positive test can strongly protect the uninfected partner. In Rwanda, condom use in discordant couples who received counseling increased from 3 to 57 percent. In Congo (the former Zaire), the increase was from 5 to 77 percent.

Comprehensive sex education in schools can promote safer sex while actually decreasing sexual activity among young people. A review of 23 school programs found that teens who received specific information and training about how to insist on condom use were less likely to engage in sex. Those who did have sex had it more safely and less frequently than those not exposed to AIDS-specific educational material. Adolescents not yet sexually active who receive information about HIV have their first sexual experiences later in life and have fewer sex partners than students who receive HIV information after they have begun having sex.

Peer influence and community action are excellent complements to more general education. In one investigation, researchers identified popular opinion leaders among gay men in small cities. The researchers trained these "trendsetters" to endorse safer sex practices among their friends and acquaintances. The number of men engaging in unprotected anal intercourse dropped by 25 percent in only two months; condom use went up 16 percent; and 18 percent fewer men had more than one sex partner. In two similar cities without such peer influences, no changes occurred. In another trendsetter study the rate of unprotected intercourse among young gay men fell by more than 50 percent. Such a drop in risk behavior could actually reduce the HIV transmission rate enough to stop the epidemic in that population.

> *"Targeted education aimed at a particular at-risk community is a prime way to persuade people to engage in preventive practices."*

Advertising and marketing can also change a community norm, making condoms more acceptable. A mass-media campaign advocating safer sex in Congo caused condom sales to increase from 800,000 in 1988 to more than 18 million by 1991. A local survey found that those claiming they practiced mutual fidelity went from 29 to 46 percent in a one-year period. An aggressive marketing campaign aimed at 17- to 30-year-olds in Switzerland saw condom use with casual sex partners rise from 8 to 50 percent between 1987 and 1991. Among 17- to 20-year-olds the figure went from 19 to 73 percent. Critics of the frank presentation of sexually oriented materials decry the potential for increasing rates of sexual activity. The Swiss study, however, found such rates to be unchanged—only the safety of the practices increased.

Easing access to condoms is another way to increase their use—both by giving them away and by making them less embarrassing to buy. A study published in 1997 in the *American Journal of Public Health* reported that when condoms were made available in high schools, usage went up without an increase in number of sex partners or a lowering of the age of initiation of sexual activity. At a drug-abuse treatment center, condoms were almost five times as likely to be taken from private rest rooms as from a public waiting area. Clearly, the perception of privacy encourages the acquisition of condoms.

Physician-patient dialogue may also help reduce risk behaviors, but doctors have squandered valuable opportunities. A recent study found that only 39 percent of adolescents ever talked with their doctors about avoiding HIV, and only 15 percent discussed their sex lives; however, almost 75 percent said they would trust their doctors with information about their sex habits, and up to 90 percent said they would find it helpful to talk about sex with a doctor. Ninety-four percent of physicians ask about smoking habits; frank discussions of sex are no less appropriate in a doctor-patient setting.

> *"A review of 23 school programs found that teens who received specific information and training about how to insist on condom use were less likely to engage in sex."*

Drug treatment should be a first-line approach to reducing risk for HIV and other infectious diseases in intravenous drug users. Substitution strategies, such as methadone treatment for heroin addiction, clearly reduce transmission of HIV through needle sharing.

Access to clean needles can help protect those still using injection drugs. Exchange programs, despite the controversies they elicit, have been shown to lower the risk of viral infection in many studies worldwide. Six U.S. government-funded studies have found that needle exchanges help to reduce HIV transmission without leading to greater drug use. Some jurisdictions have expanded beyond needle exchange. In 1992 Connecticut began a model program in which pharmacists were permitted to sell and individuals were allowed to possess up to 10 syringes without medical prescriptions. Among users who reported ever sharing syringes, sharing dropped from 52 to 31 percent, and street purchases of syringes dropped from 74 to 28 percent. Fears of encouraging drug abuse have proved unfounded: many studies have shown that needle availability does not increase the use of illegal drugs.

Direct outreach to drug users is also effective. A program supported by the National Institute on Drug Abuse followed 641 injection addicts, consistently encouraging them to seek treatment to get off drugs and use safe injection methods in the interim. After four years, 90 individuals had contracted HIV, only half the statistical expectation for that population.

What Does Not Work

One-time exposure to information is less successful than interventions that teach skills and reinforce positive behaviors repeatedly. Young people in particular need to learn exactly how to use condoms and how to be assertive about demanding their use before they will modify their behavior significantly.

A single message is insufficient to reach the multiple diverse communities grappling with the AIDS epidemic. Educational approaches must be tailored to fit the ethnicity, culture and sexual preference of a given population. The San Francisco example of outreach aimed at the gay community attests to the success of this focused approach.

Abstinence-only programs do a disservice to America's youth. Congress recently approved $250 million for five years of sex education restricted to discussions of abstinence alone. Such efforts cater to a political agenda more than any societal realities—two thirds of high school seniors say they have had intercourse. Educational programs, while encouraging abstinence, must provide the knowledge and means to protect the young from HIV.

Coercive measures to identify people with HIV or their sexual partners are likely to backfire. In this age of promising HIV therapies, it is important that infected individuals enter care as soon as possible after diagnosis. Early therapy can also prevent pregnant mothers from passing HIV to their children. But mandatory testing and the threat of coercive measures to identify sexual contacts undermine faith in and comfort with the health care system. A 1995 survey in Los Angeles found that 86 percent of those responding would have avoided an HIV test if they knew their names would be given to a government agency. Expanding opportunities for anonymous and confidential testing can bring more people into care and counseling.

> *"Easing access to condoms is another way to increase their use—both by giving them away and by making them less embarrassing to buy."*

Settling for the status quo is also a threat to prevention. Investigators need to continue to develop and refine interventions that can reach groups at risk. Women in particular need approaches that protect them from infected partners. With access to female condoms, their rates of sexually transmitted diseases are lower than when only male condoms are available. Better microbicides would likewise protect women whose partners are unwilling to practice safer sex.

Prevention is in many ways a less exciting topic than the development of wonder treatments or a vaccine. Yet effective behavioral and policy interventions are the best tools available to address an epidemic in which 16,000 people become infected worldwide every day. Concerted research on HIV vaccines must continue. Yet even when a vaccine is available, it most likely will not confer 100 percent protection on all those vaccinated. Distribution of the vaccine to everyone in need is another obstacle on the road to full protection.

Therefore, behavioral intervention will continue to play a role in bringing the global HIV epidemic under control and is indeed a matter of life and death. As June Osborn, former chair of the National Commission on AIDS, has said, "If we do preventive medicine and public health right, then nothing happens and it is very boring. We should all be praying for boredom."

Protesters attempt to educate the public. Federally funded studies have shown that needle exchanges help to lower HIV transmission without increasing drug use.

Decline in risk behavior was significant and fast because of targeted education. Reaching individual cultural groups in a manner acceptable to those populations pays prevention dividends.

Abstinence Education Will Prevent the Spread of Sexually Transmitted Diseases

by Linda Bussey

About the author: Linda Bussey is a member of the national advisory board of the Medical Institute for Sexual Health, an organization that stresses abstinence education for teens.

By the end of the 1960's, we, as a society, changed our perspective regarding a number of issues, and Congress backed the obvious change in attitudes with legislation. For example, institutional racism was recognized as wrong. Civil rights legislation was enacted to support needed social change. During the 60s, American thinking about sex changed as well. Legislation followed public opinion in supporting the "Sexual Revolution" as value-free sex education programs were funded. Turning from a clear standard of sexual abstinence before marriage, our institutions began to reflect the mantra, "If it feels good, do it." Later that mantra included, ". . . with a condom." What we didn't expect were the unintended consequences of a rising birth rate to unmarried teens and the rising incidence of sexually transmitted disease. I would like to give the medical evidence that it is time to again change our minds and to support new thinking with legislation and policy.

The Consequences of the Sexual Revolution

The past decade has brought an unprecedented epidemic of sexually transmitted disease. We have more sexually transmitted diseases affecting more individuals than ever before in medical history. Two recent studies looking at the incidence of chlamydia, a bacteria that can cause scarring of a woman's tubes and lead to infertility, were alarming. In one study of military recruits, re-

Reprinted from Linda Bussey, "Abstinence Education in Welfare Revision," testimony before the House Subcommittee on Oversight and Investigations, September 25, 1998.

searchers found nearly 1 in 10 young women tested positive for chlamydia infection with the highest incidence in the 17 year olds. In the other, researchers found one-third of adolescent girls in a Baltimore sexually transmitted disease (STD) clinic to be infected. This damaging infection brought many young women into the day surgery center where I served as medical director and attending anesthesiologist. These patients required surgery for chronic pelvic pain, for infertility often caused by pelvic inflammatory disease (PID), or to be treated for an ectopic pregnancy—a condition which has increased 600 percent in the past two decades.

Another disease that was uncommon until the mid-1980s is the human papilloma virus (HPV). This virus is the cause of thousands of abnormal pap smears, requiring treatment and follow-up. It is also the cause of over 93 percent of cases of cancer of the cervix in women and almost 5000 deaths from cervical cancer each year. A study at Rutgers University showed infection with this virus in 60 percent of the sexually active college women who were followed over a three year period. I had patients as young as 15 coming for surgical treatment to their cervix to prevent this cancer from developing. A patient's mom asked, "Would a condom have prevented this?" as her daughter was wheeled to the operating room. The truth is, studies suggest that using a condom provides almost no protection from human papilloma virus infection and the cancer it causes.

> *"We have more sexually transmitted diseases affecting more individuals than ever before in medical history."*

Genital herpes now infects 1 in 5 Americans over the age of 12. The incidence of gonorrhea is highest in 18–24 year olds. Both increase the likelihood of contracting HIV. Not surprisingly, 1 in 4 new cases of HIV occur in young people under 22 years of age. Although births to unmarried teens are down as compared to previous years, it is still widely accepted that there are almost 1 million teen births in the United States each year. The teen mothers, fathers and the babies born to them are often negatively impacted, both economically and educationally, for the rest of their lives.

A Different Approach Is Needed

The fallout on the social and medical well-being of the youth of our country has been disastrous. Clearly, it is time to change our attitudes about the message of sexuality education. In 1991, Dr. Joe McIlhaney, an obstetrician/gynecologist of Austin, Texas, and a national advisory board comprised of medical professionals and educators formed The Medical Institute for Sexual Health. His organization advocates the need for accurate medical information to better formulate public policy and educational methods to prevent the twin epidemics of nonmarital pregnancy and sexually transmitted disease.

Partnering with programs all across the nation, abstinence education began to take root in our nation's schools. Legislation followed in the Welfare Reform Act of 1997 and the definition of abstinence education was codified to include "abstinence before marriage." American teens began to change their minds about virginity, which is up 5 percent in teen girls 15–19 since 1990, and up 5 percent in teen boys since 1988. The results: No sex, no sexually transmitted disease, no pregnancy.

> *"The truth is, studies suggest that using a condom provides almost no protection from human papilloma virus infection and the cancer it causes."*

This is what character-based abstinence education is about: supportive information and skills to help kids change their minds about the prevailing cultural norm of "everybody's doing it." Character-based abstinence education helps teens to see how risky sexual practices play a role in the STD epidemic. Oral sex carries risk of disease transmission of HIV, herpes, gonorrhea and syphilis. Character-based abstinence education is not about dressing up the failed sex education programs of the last 30 years with a mixed message and calling it reality based sex education.

The best message is one with clear guidelines. Like with the battle to extend civil rights, the excuse that the message will not be embraced by all should not be an excuse not to try. Approximately 65 percent of American teens are currently abstinent, including those who have committed to the concept of secondary virginity. Secondary virginity decreases the risk of disease by decreasing number of lifetime partners and is a very healthy goal for teens who have been sexually active in the past.

When I began speaking to students around Dallas in the early 90s, I would begin by asking, "What is safe sex?" They would all shout "Condoms!" In 1998, the answer is another chorus. "Abstinence" is clearly a message kids, adolescents and young adults are dying to hear—in some cases literally.

Our thanks for giving us the support to help Americans change their attitudes about sexuality education.

Condoms Can Reduce the Risk of Contracting Sexually Transmitted Diseases

by Tamar Nordenberg

About the author: *Tamar Nordenberg is a staff writer for* FDA Consumer.

What do condoms have in common with toothpaste and toilet paper?

Not enough, according to Adam Glickman, owner of the Condomania stores in New York and Los Angeles. Glickman, who has sold condoms by the millions to individuals and organizations such as the Peace Corps and Planned Parenthood, says condoms should be viewed as ordinary, like toothpaste and toilet paper. "People have gotten past asking, 'Isn't brushing my teeth every morning a hassle?' Given the world we live in, wearing condoms is something you just have to do, like brushing your teeth. The stakes are too high."

Luis Lopez knows first-hand what's at stake. About 10 years ago, Lopez, now 31 and a health educator with the People With AIDS Coalition of New York, became infected with the HIV virus, which causes AIDS, during a casual sexual encounter.

"I thought people with AIDS had purple spots or looked really skinny," Lopez says. "I thought by being discriminating about who I slept with, I could keep myself safe. We know now that makes no sense."

We know now that abstaining from sex is the only foolproof protection from the sexual passage of HIV and other sexually transmitted diseases (STDs). We know, too, that for those who choose to have sex with someone who has any chance of being infected, using a latex condom during every sexual encounter can significantly reduce the risk of HIV and other sexually transmitted diseases, while protecting against pregnancy.

For those who can't or won't use latex condoms, the Food and Drug Adminis-

Reprinted from Tamar Nordenberg, "Condoms: Barriers to Bad News," *FDA Consumer*, March/April 1998.

tration (FDA) has cleared two alternative barrier methods of birth control, a male condom made of polyurethane and a condom that is worn by the woman. Both help protect against pregnancy and may provide some level of protection from STDs.

Life-Saving Barrier

A male condom, sometimes called a "rubber" or "prophylactic," is a sheath that fits snugly over a man's erect penis, with a closed end to catch the sperm and stop them from entering the woman's vagina. No prescription is needed to buy a condom.

Data show that if a condom is used correctly with every act of sexual intercourse for one year, about three out of every 100 women are expected to get pregnant.

Besides sperm, latex condoms act as a barrier to a wide variety of viruses, bacteria, and other infectious particles. By preventing contact with many sores and minimizing the exchange of infectious fluids, condoms can help prevent the transmission of sexually transmitted diseases, including HIV, gonorrhea, chlamydia, syphilis, herpes infection, and genital ulcers. Even though sperm are enormous compared to HIV, both are much too small to see. But even HIV, which is among the tiniest of STD organisms, cannot pass through a latex condom.

"Using a latex condom during every sexual encounter can significantly reduce the risk of HIV and other sexually transmitted diseases."

Millions of Americans are infected with these diseases each year, and hundreds of thousands of them become seriously ill or die as a result. According to the Centers for Disease Control and Prevention (CDC), in the United States, someone is infected with HIV every 13 minutes. CDC estimates that 65 percent of these AIDS cases can be attributed to sexual contact.

The best protection from such diseases is to not have sex or to have a mutually monogamous relationship with someone who is known to be uninfected. However, for those who are sexually active, studies have shown that proper and consistent use of latex condoms is the best defense.

A 1994 European study published in the *New England Journal of Medicine* looked at HIV transmission rates of heterosexual couples with one HIV-infected partner. The study compared the transmission rates for couples who used condoms consistently to those who didn't. Of the 123 couples who consistently used condoms, none of the HIV-free partners became infected during the study, whereas 12 of the 122 partners who didn't consistently use condoms became infected.

"The scientific evidence is compelling," says Herbert Peterson, M.D., chief of CDC's women's health and fertility branch. "We're not guessing about this."

The spermicide nonoxynol-9, used in some condoms, has been shown to be effective as a contraceptive, and may reduce the risk of transmitting certain STDs. But the spermicide has not been proven to prevent sexual transmission of HIV.

Similarly, lambskin (or natural membrane) condoms, while effective for contraception, should not be used for disease protection because the naturally occurring pores in lambskin are large enough to allow some viruses to pass through.

Hole Check

Since 1976, FDA has regulated condoms to ensure their safety and effectiveness. Currently, manufacturers of American-made and imported condoms electronically test each condom for holes and other defects. Also, before distributing the condoms to retailers, manufacturers perform additional testing on random condoms from each batch, usually involving a "water leak" test to find holes and an "air burst" test to check condom strength.

FDA oversees the testing procedures by periodically inspecting the manufacturing facilities, and the agency tests some condoms in its own laboratories to confirm their quality.

Condoms are sold in various colors, shapes or packaging to suit different personal preferences. But, whether they glow in the dark or taste like strawberries, products that sufficiently resemble a condom must comply with FDA's requirements, even if they are labeled as "novelties." The only condom-like products that need not comply are those that can't be used like condoms. For example, some novelty products have the closed end removed or are sealed so they can't be unrolled.

Correct and Consistent

Although condoms are generally expected to break less than 2 percent of the time—with more than half of the breakages occurring before ejaculation—real-life pregnancy rates over a year of condom use may be as high as 15 percent.

Inconsistent or incorrect use of condoms explains the discrepancy, according to Lillian Yin, director of the division in FDA that regulates condoms and other reproductive devices. One national survey of heterosexual adults with multiple sex partners found that only 17 percent used a condom every time they had sex.

"Using condoms consistently is a start, but using them correctly is another key to protecting oneself."

"People say they use condoms," Yin says, "but do they use them each and every time and use them correctly? That's another ball game. We hear it all the time—'We tried to use it, but. . . .'"

But what? Partner trust was the most-cited reason for not wearing condoms in a recent study sponsored by the National Institutes of Health (NIH). But be careful, CDC cautions, because even a trustworthy partner could unknowingly have a sexually transmitted disease.

Many participants in the NIH study said they didn't always wear a condom because sex feels better without them. Lopez responds, "If you don't use them, you run the risk of something that feels much worse."

Sometimes a couple can't use a latex condom because one partner is allergic to latex. For these people, FDA has approved condoms made from polyurethane.

If a man objects to wearing a condom for some other reason, Planned Parenthood suggests possible replies. For example, to the partner who says, "I guess you don't really love me," the organization suggests responding, "I do, but I'm not risking my future to prove it." If the man still chooses not to wear a condom, the Reality female condom cleared by FDA in 1993 offers an alternative.

Using condoms consistently is a start, but using them correctly is another key to protecting oneself. User error, not poor condom quality, leads to most breakages. But a few simple rules can minimize breaks and leaks.

Even when used correctly, condoms aren't perfect, CDC acknowledges, comparing them to other important safety-enhancing behaviors like wearing seatbelts and bicycle helmets. Imperfect as they are, condoms can significantly reduce the rates of unintended pregnancies and sexually transmitted diseases.

"Correct and consistent condom use," says CDC's Peterson, "could break the back of the AIDS epidemic."

Condoms Do Not Provide Adequate Protection from Sexually Transmitted Diseases

by Katherine Dowling

About the author: *Katherine Dowling is a family physician at the University of Southern California School of Medicine.*

The ad shows a vibrant young woman at the beach, arm in arm with a handsome man, and the small disclaimer to the left of the photo reads that the product may cause all sorts of damage to oneself and one's offspring. Do you believe for a moment that this cigarette ad seeks to discourage smoking among adolescents?

Cigarette ads can easily be compared to condom ads. The silent message for teens is that such products are available to the sophisticated and that if you're not using them, somehow you're just not "with it." If we truly wanted to discourage an activity, be it drinking, smoking, or adolescent sexual activity, the last thing in the world we would do is advertise where and how to procure the means for this activity. As a physician, I must agree with the church that condom ads will have the effect of encouraging premature sexuality in subtle ways, and will ultimately do more harm than good in terms of disease prevention through boosting the numbers of sexually active youth.

Let me tell you about one of my patients who gave a story I'm only too familiar with. I do not know if she used condoms, but given their failure rate, the point is moot. She was the same age as my own daughter, and she sat on the edge of her chair in my office crying angry tears. Her pelvic pain, caused by a germ called Chlamydia trachomatis, was sexually transmitted and is a common cause of female sterility. I gave her the standard advice: her boyfriend needed to be treated, and it would be better not to have sex until he was treated. If she had to, use a condom.

Reprinted from Katherine Dowling, "Condoms Won't Keep Our Teens Safe," *U.S. Catholic*, January 1995. Reprinted with permission from *U.S. Catholic*.

She looked me in the eyes with a sneer. I had just told her, indirectly, that her only sexual partner had betrayed her, that she may never be able to have children, and that he wouldn't suffer at all from this episode and probably didn't even know he was infected. Now I was suggesting she risk her future a second time with a flimsy condom? Did I think she was foolish enough to ever look at that guy again, much less have sex with him?

The Message That Free Condoms Send

The party line on condoms is that they are the mainstay in our defense against sexually transmitted diseases, especially AIDS. Condoms should therefore be made available in all places where persons who may be inclined to be sexually active are to be found. Based on the theory that teens are at highest risk for a little hanky-panky when things get dull and can't be expected to have the savoir faire or the cash to go to the local pharmacy, many school systems make condoms available at school, courtesy of the local taxpayers. In some cases, teens who don't accept condoms feel they may be ridiculed for not getting a piece of the action, so they take condoms whether or not they intend to use them.

What is the message here—that sexual activity outside of marriage is not only socially acceptable but also expected of the normal teenager? If authority figures determine that adolescents must have condom availability, the corollary must be that teens should be having intercourse. Our surgeon general has stated in an interview that our society is too Victorian, that sexual activity, apparently regardless of marital status, is a normal pleasure, but that "babies shouldn't be having babies."

"Condom ads will have the effect of encouraging premature sexuality in subtle ways, and will ultimately do more harm than good in terms of disease prevention."

How to reconcile these seemingly contradictory beliefs? Condoms with the backup of taxpayer-funded abortions? Then we can have our cake and eat it, too. Unfortunately the surgeon general hasn't taken care of patients for a long time, so she doesn't see what I as a clinician see: the guilt and heartbreak of a long-ago abortion still poisoning one's life, and the horror of a diagnosis of AIDS gotten from one's first-ever sexual partner who "seemed so wonderful."

Supporters of the promotion of condom use would have Americans believe that sex is recreation, not an integral part of the sacred bond of marriage. Just as when one is playing football one wears a mouthpiece and helmet, so one wears a condom for the sport of intercourse.

Safe Sex?

Let's take a look at how safe condoms actually are. Several studies have looked at the physical properties of semen, lubricants, and condoms; the motivation of teenagers, adults, and those using substances such as alcohol and cocaine that impair judgment; and people's ability to put a condom on correctly, use it at the right time, and take it off properly. In one study done with heterosexual couples, one partner was AIDS-virus positive and one was negative at the beginning of the study. These couples were using condoms consistently, yet close to 2 percent transferred the virus to the uninfected partner. Fifteen percent of similar couples who did not always use condoms correctly transferred the virus to the uninfected partner over the course of several years.

> *"Condoms don't usually prevent HPV transmission."*

Now let's generalize these statistics to the more than 25 million teens who would so blithely be protected with condoms. Assume that less than 50 percent are sexually active, say 10 million for the sake of making the math easier. If all these teens had only one teen partner and used condoms all the time and properly, 100,000 would transfer the AIDS virus from a theoretically infected to an uninfected partner. Of course most teens are not infected with the AIDS virus. However, AIDS is not the only problem condoms are touted as preventing.

Another problem that all sexually active heterosexual couples are exposed to is an unexpected pregnancy. The failure rate for condoms is at least 10 percent.

And then we have venereal diseases. Detected venereal diseases number in the millions each year, 33,000 each day in the U.S. alone. The germs that cause venereal diseases are smaller than spermatozoa, so the failure rate of condoms in preventing these is even higher. Many venereal diseases are not even detected, especially in males, who may transmit them to several female partners (and vice versa, of course, but less commonly).

What's so bad about venereal diseases? Won't a shot of penicillin kill these bugs? Unfortunately, often not. Some destroy the female organs, making childbearing impossible, and all the unfortunate woman may feel is some pelvic discomfort—maybe not enough to make her seek medical care until she finds she is unable to conceive. Other venereal diseases are associated with cancer, like the infamous human papillomavirus (HPV), which also causes genital warts. And condoms don't usually prevent HPV transmission. Add to that the fact that some gonorrhea strains, which cause pelvic inflammatory disease and sterility, are becoming resistant to penicillin and other antibiotics.

Defects

Back to the condoms themselves. First off, 4 out of every 1,000 manufactured condoms are permitted by the Food and Drug Administration (FDA) to have water leaks. Now the waterleak test will allow detection of holes in the condom of 5 microns. Five microns is 48 times bigger than the AIDS virus and 119 times bigger than the hepatitis B virus, another sexually transmitted germ. It's also considerably bigger than the chlamydia and gonorrhea germs, which makes one suspect that when the surgeon general espouses sex with condoms, what she is really trying to prevent is pregnancy.

Another test on condoms done by the Mariposa Foundation found that 18 out of 70 popular brands of condoms leaked the AIDS virus. And the FDA found that about 10 percent of production lots of U.S. condoms did not meet FDA standards.

Many people feel that it's impossible to stop kids from having sex, even if we wanted to. My reply is that society itself has failed to give our teens appropriate reinforcement for chaste behavior. In fact, it does the exact opposite—just watch one episode of *Melrose Place*.

Back in 1950, unmarried teens had babies at a rate of 59.2 per 1,000. Remember, abortions were more difficult to get and, hence, less frequent in those days. In 1989, the number of live births to teens was 347.9 per 1,000, close to a six-fold increase over 40 years. Add to this the fact that more than 40 percent of pregnant teens abort their babies these days and that birth control is more available and effective than four decades ago, and you have only two explanations for the inferred changes in sexual behavior: either teen hormone production has increased drastically, or society no longer holds teens and others to certain standards of behavior that in this day and age could be lifesaving.

Stressing Responsibility

What should schools, parents, and society be teaching kids about sex? From my perspective, responsibility needs to be stressed. There's nothing wrong in teaching the physiology of sex, but the humanity of the fetus needs to be stressed as well. The young must be told that sex means something different to boys than it does to girls. They need to understand that when it comes to having a long-lasting marriage, compatibility in the bedroom is far less important than compatibility across the kitchen table, that it is not their right to have sex when and where they feel like it any more than it is their right to drive an auto without a license.

Most of all, we must media-proof our children. They must be taught to steel their minds against the incessant messages of TV, magazines, and radio that sex is inevitable and desirable for adolescents. Somewhere we must come up with the courage to see the beauty and desirability of chastity as being a virtue of the strong. Now how can we possibly get this message across at the same time we peddle those thin rubber balloons we call condoms?

As a physician and a mother, it is apparent to me that my generation has failed the next generation miserably, and in some cases, I fear, fatally. Society needs to reclaim itself by guiding our teens and young adults to espouse the proper use of sex as a God-given gift intended to bind couples in marriage through mutual spiritual communication and pleasure for their benefit and that of their offspring.

And besides, there are a whole lot of leaky condoms out there!

Needle Exchange Programs Prevent the Spread of HIV

by Stephen Chapman

About the author: *Stephen Chapman is a syndicated columnist on the staff of the* Chicago Tribune.

The AIDS epidemic has unleashed a slew of efforts to stop transmission of the virus—from distributing condoms to teenagers to tightly screening blood transfusions. But, for years, one of the most effective and inexpensive weapons has languished on the shelf: needle exchange. In December 1996, the Clinton administration recommended additional money for AIDS research, but barely mentioned needle exchange. The neglect comes at a price: though the virus has abated among gay men, it has proliferated among intravenous drug users, their sexual partners and their children. According to the Centers for Disease Control (CDC), this group now accounts for a full third of new HIV infections—up from just 12 percent in 1981. The news gets worse. Unlike other groups, addicts are often cut off from new treatments because of cost or regimen. So, while some hail the coming end of the epidemic, for drug addicts the plague is just entering a new phase.

President Clinton could change all of this. Although current law prohibits federal funds for clean-syringe programs, the executive branch can lift the ban if it finds that needle exchanges slow the spread of AIDS without promoting more drug use. Clinton, facing an election in 1996, refused to do so. But in 1997, he had no political pretext. He was not only free of election pressures but Congress had handed him the perfect opportunity: it instructed the administration to report by February 15 on the efficacy of needle exchange. When the long-awaited report from the Department of Health and Human Services (HHS) arrived, it declared the obvious: needle exchanges do indeed combat HIV transmission. Yet, in classic Clintonesque style, the president straddled, saying such programs may or may not encourage drug use. HHS hailed the report as a change in policy. Meanwhile, the ban on federal funding remains in place.

Needle-exchange advocates were understandably upset. "I'd say they mugwumped—you know, mug on one side of the fence, wump on the other," says Dave Purchase, head of the North American Syringe Exchange Network in Tacoma, Washington. "The scientists have spoken on this issue. It's time for the politicians to catch up," adds Dan Bigg, who runs Chicago's largest program. Bigg says he's $130,000 short of what he needs to keep his program going this year. Opening the federal tap even a little would help a lot.

The Reasons for Needle Exchange

A little more than a decade ago, needle-exchange programs began to provide sterile hypodermic syringes to drug users. The first exchange was started in Boston in 1986, and the idea soon spread to San Francisco and other cities. Often the programs defied state laws requiring a prescription to obtain a syringe and treating possession of them, except for medical purposes, as a crime. But they soon won the blessing of many mayors and police chiefs, who were willing to look the other way rather than discard a weapon against AIDS. There are now some 111 needle-exchange programs in the United States and Puerto Rico, from the biggest cities to smaller urban areas such as Rockford, Illinois, and Fairbanks, Alaska; together, they collect and distribute some 10 million syringes every year.

The initial theory behind the exchanges remains unchanged: that addicts share their needles not because they want to but because they have to. Since laws banning over-the-counter sale of syringes made the devices scarce, drug users learned to hoard, re-use and share them—even after the emergence and spread of AIDS made this potentially fatal. Grant them cheap or free access to sterile injecting equipment, activists argued, and many users would act with more regard for self-preservation. But opponents contended that anyone eager to put heroin in his arm was unlikely to be terribly fastidious about what he used to inject it. Offering addicts access to clean syringes at low or no cost, they maintained, would do little to slow the epidemic and would foster more drug addiction by signaling society's indulgence of such behavior.

Both theories were entirely plausible, but only one has turned out to be right. In recent years, one study after another has reached the same conclusion. The most definitive one was a

> *"While some hail the coming end of the [AIDS] epidemic, for drug addicts the plague is just entering a new phase."*

report released in September 1995 by the National Academy of Sciences' National Research Council, which concluded that "well-implemented needle exchange programs can be effective in preventing the spread of HIV and do not increase the use of illegal drugs." The council endorsed an end to the federal funding ban and proposed repealing state prescription and drug paraphernalia laws that make syringes scarce.

But the Clinton administration has apparently decided that the political price of endorsing needle exchange outweighs any lives the programs might save. Certainly, there is no potent lobby for drug addicts. And Republicans would doubtless portray a reversal as proof of Clinton's permissive attitude toward drug use. So inaction prevails. After a federally financed study by researchers at the University of California at San Francisco (UCSF) gave a strong endorsement to such programs in 1993, HHS asked scientists at the CDC to review the study and make their own recommendations—which turned out to be identical to those of the UCSF panel. HHS, finding the results unsatisfactory, simply declined to release the CDC analysis, even after it was leaked to the *Washington Post*.

> *"Well-implemented needle exchange programs can be effective in preventing the spread of HIV and do not increase the use of illegal drugs."*

President Clinton will never have a more auspicious opportunity to take the modest risk of giving his blessing to needle exchange. The ferocity of drug czar Barry McCaffrey has largely insulated the president from any charge of being soft on drugs. And Clinton can offer needle exchange as a way not only to prevent AIDS, but to funnel addicts into treatment programs—a claim that has the virtue of being true. Besides sterile equipment, most needle-exchange providers offer counseling and drug treatment referrals.

Saving Lives

Lifting the ban can be easily justified to the public as a simple matter of saving lives, not just of drug users, but of their innocent spouses and children. Here Clinton can count on the backing of public health experts. A recent article in the British medical journal the *Lancet* by Peter Lurie, a physician at the Center for AIDS Research at the UCSF, and Ernest Drucker, an epidemiologist at Montefiore Medical Center/Albert Einstein College of Medicine in New York, estimates that, if the United States had begun widely promoting clean syringes in 1987, as Australia did, it could have prevented between 4,000 and 10,000 HIV infections between 1987 and 1995. By 2000, another 11,000 might [have been] averted. Clinton can also defend the policy change on unsentimental fiscal grounds, since the aversion to clean-needle programs costs society a lot of money. Preventing a single HIV transmission through syringe exchanges, according to the 1993 UCSF study, costs between $3,773 and $12,000. Repealing prescription and drug paraphernalia laws offers an even better payoff, since many addicts are more than willing to spend their own cash on sterile equipment. Caring for an AIDS patient, by contrast, means an average expense of some $119,000—a cost that usually falls on taxpayers.

After the 1995 White House conference on AIDS, one attendee expressed pleasant surprise at hearing President Clinton denounce homophobia, but said it would be nice to hear him mention clean needles as well. For the president to ignore the value of needle exchange in combating AIDS is to invite a harsh historical judgment: that he knew what needed to be done but, for flimsy political reasons, refused to do it. For the likely victims of AIDS, of course, the consequences will be even worse.

Needle Exchange Programs Do Not Prevent the Spread of HIV

by Joe Loconte

About the author: *Joe Loconte is deputy editor of* Policy Review.

In a midrise office building on Manhattan's West 37th Street, about two blocks south of the Port Authority bus terminal, sits the Positive Health Project, one of 11 needle-exchange outlets in New York City. This particular neighborhood, dotted by X-rated video stores, peep shows, and a grimy hot dog stand, could probably tolerate some positive health. But it's not clear that's what the program's patrons are getting.

The clients are intravenous (IV) drug users. They swap their used needles for clean ones and, it is hoped, avoid the AIDS virus, at least until their next visit. There's no charge, no hassles, no meddlesome questions. That's just the way Walter, a veteran heroin user, likes it.

"Just put me on an island and don't mess with me," he says, lighting up a cigarette.

A tall, thinnish man, Walter seems weary for his 40-some years. Like many of the estimated 250,000 IV drug users in this city, he has spent years shooting up and has bounced in and out of detoxification programs. "Don't get the idea in your mind you're going to control it," he says. "I thought I could control it. But dope's a different thing. You just want it." Can he imagine his life without drugs? "I'm past that," he says, his face tightening. "The only good thing I do is getting high."

Heroin First, Then Breathing

Supporters of needle-exchange programs (NEPs), from AIDS activists to Secretary of Health and Human Services Donna Shalala, seem to have reached the same verdict on Walter's life. They take his drug addiction as a given, but want

Excerpted from Joe Loconte, "Killing Them Softly," *Policy Review*, July/August 1998. Reprinted with permission from *Policy Review*.

to keep him free of HIV by making sure he isn't borrowing dirty syringes. Says Shalala, "This is another life-saving intervention." That message is gaining currency, thanks in part to at least 112 programs in 29 states, distributing millions of syringes each year. Critics say free needles just make it easier for addicts to go about their business: abusing drugs. Ronn Constable, a Brooklynite who used heroin and cocaine for nearly 20 years, says he would have welcomed the needle-exchange program—for saving him money. "An addict doesn't want to spend a dollar on anything else but his drugs," he says.

Do needle exchanges, then, save lives or fuel addiction? . . .

Joined by much of the scientific community, the Clinton administration has tacitly embraced a profoundly misguided notion: that we must not confront drug abusers on moral or religious grounds. Instead, we should use medical interventions to minimize the harm their behavior invites. Directors of needle-exchange outlets pride themselves on running "nonjudgmental" programs. While insisting they do not encourage illegal drug use, suppliers distribute "safe crack kits" explaining the best ways to inject crack cocaine. Willie Easterlins, an outreach worker at a needle-stocked van in Brooklyn, sums up the philosophy this way: "I have to give you a needle. I can't judge," he says. "That's the first thing they teach us."

"Most IV drug users . . . die not from HIV-tainted needles but from other health problems, overdoses, or homicide."

This approach, however well intentioned, ignores the soul-controlling darkness of addiction and the moral freefall that sustains it. "When addicts talk about enslavement, they're not exaggerating," says Terry Horton, the medical director of Phoenix House, one of the nation's largest residential treatment centers. "It is their first and foremost priority. Heroin first, then breathing, then food."

It is true that needle-sharing among intravenous (IV) drug users is a major source of HIV transmission, and that the incidence of HIV is rising most rapidly among this group—a population of more than a million people. Last year, about 30 percent of all new HIV infections were linked to IV drug use. The Clinton administration is correct to call this a major public-health risk.

Nevertheless, NEP advocates seem steeped in denial about the behavioral roots of the crisis, conduct left unchallenged by easy access to clean syringes. Most IV drug users, in fact, die not from HIV-tainted needles but from other health problems, overdoses, or homicide. By evading issues of personal responsibility, the White House and its NEP allies are neglecting the most effective help for drug abusers: enrollment in tough-minded treatment programs enforced by drug courts. Moreover, in the name of "saving lives," they seem prepared to surrender countless addicts to life on the margins—an existence of scheming, scamming, disease, and premature death.

Curious Science

Over the last decade, NEPs have secured funding from local departments of public health to establish outlets in 71 cities. But that may be as far as their political argument will take them: Federal law prohibits federal money from flowing to the programs until it can be proved they prevent AIDS without encouraging drug use.

It's no surprise, then, that advocates are trying to enlist science as an ally. They claim that numerous studies of NEPs prove they are effective. Says Sandra Thurman, the director of the Office of National AIDS Policy, "There is very little doubt that these programs reduce HIV transmission." In arguing for federal funding, a White House panel on AIDS recently cited "clear scientific evidence of the efficacy of such programs."

> *"The data simply do not, and for methodological reasons probably cannot, provide clear evidence that needle exchanges decrease HIV infection rates."*

The studies, though suggestive, prove no such thing. Activists tout the results of a New Haven, Connecticut, study, published in the *American Journal of Medicine*, saying the program reduces HIV among participants by a third. Not exactly. Researchers tested needles from anonymous users—not the addicts themselves—to see if they contained HIV. They never measured "seroconversion rates," the portion of participants who became HIV positive during the study. Even Peter Lurie, a University of Michigan researcher and avid NEP advocate, admits that "the validity of testing of syringes is limited." A likely explanation for the decreased presence of HIV in syringes, according to scientists, is sampling error.

Another significant report was published in 1993 by the University of California and funded by the U.S. Centers for Disease Control. A panel reviewed 21 studies on the impact of NEPs on HIV infection rates. But the best the authors could say for the programs was that none showed a higher prevalence of HIV among program clients.

Even those results don't mean much. Panel members rated the scientific quality of the studies on a five-point scale: one meant "not valid," three "acceptable," and five "excellent." Only two of the studies earned ratings of three or higher. Of those, neither showed a reduction in HIV levels. No wonder the authors concluded that the data simply do not, and for methodological reasons probably cannot, provide clear evidence that needle exchanges decrease HIV infection rates.

The Missing Link

The most extensive review of needle-exchange studies was commissioned in 1993 by the U.S. Department of Health and Human Services (HHS), which directed the National Academy of Sciences (NAS) to oversee the project. Their report, "Preventing HIV Transmission: The Role of Sterile Needles and Bleach," was issued in 1995 and set off a political firestorm.

"Well-implemented needle-exchange programs can be effective in preventing the spread of HIV and do not increase the use of illegal drugs," a 15-member panel concluded. It recommended lifting the ban on federal funding for NEPs, along with laws against possession of injection paraphernalia. The NAS report has emerged as the bible for true believers of needle exchange.

It is not likely to stand the test of time. A truly scientific trial testing the ability of NEPs to reduce needle-sharing and HIV transmission would set up two similar, randomly selected populations of drug users. One group would be given access to free needles, the other would not. Researchers would follow them for at least a year, taking periodic blood tests.

None of the studies reviewed by NAS researchers, however, were designed in this way. Their methodological problems are legion: Sample sizes are often too small to be statistically meaningful. Participants are self-selected, so that the more health-conscious could be skewing the results. As many as 60 percent of study participants drop out. And researchers rely on self-reporting, a notoriously untrustworthy tool.

"Nobody has done the basic science yet," says David Murray, the research director of the Statistical Assessment Service, a watchdog group in Washington, D.C. "If this were the FDA applying the standard for a new drug, they would [block] it right there."

> *"Though it boasts the largest needle-exchange program in North America, Vancouver is straining under an AIDS epidemic."*

The NAS panel admitted its conclusions were not based on reviews of well-designed trials. Such studies, the authors agreed, simply do not exist. Not to worry, they said: "The limitations of individual studies do not necessarily preclude us from being able to reach scientifically valid conclusions." When all of the studies are considered together, they argued, the results are compelling.

"That's like tossing a bunch of broken Christmas ornaments in a box and claiming you have something nice and new and usable," Murray says. "What you have is a lot of broken ornaments." Two of the three physicians on the NAS panel, Lawrence Brown and Herbert Kleber, agree. They deny their report established anything like a scientific link between lower HIV rates and needle exchanges. "The existing data is flawed," says Kleber, executive vice president for medical research at Columbia University. "NEPs may, in theory, be effective, but the data doesn't prove that they are."

Some needle-exchange advocates acknowledge the dearth of hard science. Don Des Jarlais, a researcher at New York's Beth Israel Medical Center, writes in a 1996 report that "there has been no direct evidence that participation is associated with a lower risk" of HIV infection. Lurie, writing in the *American*

Journal of Epidemiology, says that "no one study, on its own, should be used to declare the programs effective." Nevertheless, supporters insist, the "pattern of evidence" is sufficient to march ahead with the programs.

Mixed Results

That argument might make sense if all the best studies created a happy, coherent picture. They don't. In fact, more-recent and better-controlled studies cast serious doubt on the ability of NEPs to reduce HIV infection.

In 1996, Vancouver researchers followed 1,006 intravenous cocaine and heroin users who visited needle exchanges, conducting periodic blood tests and interviews. The results, published in the British research journal *AIDS,* were not encouraging: About 40 percent of the test group reported borrowing a used needle in the preceding six months. Worse, after only eight months, 18.6 percent of those initially HIV negative became infected with the virus.

Dr. Steffanie Strathdee, of the British Columbia Centre for Excellence in HIV/AIDS, was the report's lead researcher. She found it "particularly disturbing" that needle-sharing among program participants, despite access to clean syringes, is common. Though an NEP advocate, Strathdee concedes that the high HIV rates are "alarming." Shepherd Smith, founder of Americans for a Sound AIDS/HIV Policy, says that compared to similar drug-using populations in the United States, the Vancouver results are "disastrous."

Though it boasts the largest needle-exchange program in North America, Vancouver is straining under an AIDS epidemic. When its NEP began in 1988, HIV prevalence among IV drug users was less than 2 percent. Today it's about 23 percent, despite a citywide program that dispenses 2.5 million needles a year.

A 1997 Montreal study is even more troubling. It showed that addicts who used needle exchanges were more than twice as likely to become infected with HIV as those who didn't. Published in the *American Journal of Epidemiology*, the report found that 33 percent of NEP users and 13 percent of nonusers became infected during the study period. Moreover, about three out of four program clients continued to share needles, roughly the same rate as nonparticipants.

The results are hard to dismiss. The report, though it did not rely on truly random selection, is the most sophisticated attempt so far to overcome the weaknesses of previous NEP studies. Researchers worked with a statistically significant sample (about 1,500), established test groups with better controls and lower dropout rates, and took greater care to account for "confounding variables." They followed each participant for an average of 21 months, taking blood samples every six months.

> *"'People think that everybody in shooting galleries worries about AIDS or syphilis or crack-addicted babies. That's the least of people's worries.'"*

Blood samples don't lie. Attending an NEP was "a strong predictor" of the risk of contracting HIV, according to Julie Bruneau of the University of Montreal, the lead researcher. Bruneau's team then issued a warning: "We believe caution is warranted before accepting NEPs as uniformly beneficial in any setting." . . .

Death-Defying Logic

Critics of needle exchanges are forced to admit there's a certain logic to the concept, at least in theory: Give enough clean needles to an IV drug user and he won't bum contaminated "spikes" when he wants a fix.

But ex-addicts themselves, and the medical specialists who treat them, say it isn't that simple. "People think that everybody in shooting galleries worries about AIDS or syphilis or crack-addicted babies. That's the least of people's worries," says Jean Scott, the director of adult programs at Phoenix House in Manhattan. "While they're using, all they can think about is continuing to use and where they're going to get their next high."

> *"There just isn't much evidence, scientific or otherwise, that free drug paraphernalia is protecting users."*

Indeed, the NEP crowd mistakenly assumes that most addicts worry about getting AIDS. Most probably don't: The psychology and physiology of addiction usually do not allow them the luxury. "Once they start pumping their system with drugs, judgment disappears. Memory disappears. Nutrition disappears. The ability to evaluate their life needs disappears," says Eric Voth, the chairman of the International Drug Strategy Institute and one of the nation's leading addiction specialists. "What makes anybody think they'll make clean needles a priority?"

Ronn Constable, now a program director at Teen Challenge International in New York, says his addiction consumed him 24 hours a day, seven days a week. Addicts call it "chasing the bag": shooting up, feeling the high, and planning the next hit before withdrawal. "For severe addicts, that's all they do," Constable says. "Their whole life is just scheming to get their next dollar to get their next bundle of dope.". . .

Name Your Poison

In the debate over federal funding for NEPs, herein lies their siren song: Clean needles save lives. But there just isn't much evidence, scientific or otherwise, that free drug paraphernalia is protecting users.

The reason is drug addiction. Addicts attending NEPs continue to swap needles and engage in risky sexual behavior. All the studies that claim otherwise are based on self-reporting, an unreliable gauge.

By not talking much about drug abuse, NEP activists effectively sidestep the desperation created by addiction. When drug users run out of money for their habit, for example, they often turn to prostitution—no matter how many clean needles are in the cupboard. And the most common way of contracting HIV is, of course, sexual intercourse. "Sex is a currency in the drug world," says Horton of Phoenix House. "It is a major mode of HIV infection. And you don't address that with needle exchange."

At least a third of the women in treatment at the Brooklyn Teen Challenge had been lured into prostitution. About 15 percent of the female clients in Manhattan's Phoenix House contracted HIV by exchanging sex for drugs. In trying to explain the high HIV rates in Vancouver, researchers admitted "it may be that sexual transmission plays an important role."

Kleber, a psychiatrist and a leading addiction specialist, has been treating drug abusers for 30 years. He says NEPs, even those that offer education and health services, aren't likely to become beacons of behavior modification. "Addiction erodes your ability to change your behavior," he says. "And NEPs have no track record of changing risky sexual behavior.". . .

Good and Ready?

Keeping drug users free of AIDS is a noble—but narrow—goal. Surely the best hope of keeping them alive is to get them off drugs and into treatment. Research from the National Institute for Drug Abuse (NIDA) shows that untreated opiate addicts die at a rate seven to eight times higher than similar patients in methadone-based treatment programs.

Needle suppliers claim they introduce addicts to rehab services, and Shalala wants local officials to include treatment referral in any new needle-exchange programs. But program staffers are not instructed to confront addicts about their drug habit. The assumption: Unless drug abusers are ready to quit on their own, it won't work.

This explains why NEP advocates smoothly assert they support drug treatment, yet gladly supply users with all the drug-injection equipment they need. "The idea that they will

> *"[Needle-exchange programs] offer no remedy for the ravages of drug addiction."*

choose on their own when they're ready is nonsense," says Voth, who says he's treated perhaps 5,000 abusers of cocaine, heroin, and crack. "Judgment is one of the things that disappears with addiction. The worst addicts are the ones least likely to stumble into sobriety and treatment."

According to health officials, most addicts do not seek treatment voluntarily, but enter through the criminal-justice system. Even those who volunteer do so because of intense pressure from spouses or employers or raw physical pain from deteriorating health. In other words, they begin to confront some of the unpleasant consequences of their drug habit.

"The only way a drug addict is going to consider stopping is by experiencing pain," says Robert Dupont, a clinical professor of psychiatry at Georgetown University Medical School. "Pain is what helps to break their delusion," says

David Batty, the director of Teen Challenge in Brooklyn. "The faster they real-ize they're on a dead-end street, the faster they see the need to change.". . .

Reducing Harm

Needle-exchange advocates chafe at the thought of coercing drug users into treatment. This signals perhaps their most grievous omission: They refuse to challenge the self-absorption that nourishes drug addiction.

In medical terms, it's called "harm reduction"—accept the irresponsible be-havior and try to minimize its effects with health services and education. Some needle exchanges, for example, distribute guides to safer drug use. A pamphlet from an NEP in Bridgeport, Connecticut, explains how to prepare crack cocaine for injection. It then urges users to "take care of your veins. Rotate injection sites. . . ."

"Harm reduction is the policy manifestation of the addict's personal wish," says psychiatrist Sally Satel, "which is to use drugs without consequences." The concept is backed by numerous medical and scientific groups, including the American Medical Association, the American Public Health Association, and the National Academy of Sciences.

In legal terms, harm reduction means the decriminalization of drug use. Legal-ization advocates, from financier George Soros to the Drug Policy Foundation, are staunch needle-exchange supporters. San Francisco mayor Willie Brown, who presides over perhaps the nation's busiest needle programs, is a leading voice in the harm-reduction chorus. "It is time," he has written, "to stop allowing moral or religious tradition to define our approach to a medical emergency."

It is time, rather, to stop medicalizing what is fundamentally a moral problem. Treatment communities that stress abstinence, responsibility, and moral re-newal, backed up by tough law enforcement, are the best hope for addicts to es-cape drugs and adopt safer, healthier lifestyles.

Despite different approaches, therapeutic communities share at least one goal: drug-free living. Though they commonly regard addiction as a disease, they all insist that addicts take full responsibility for their cure. Program directors aren't afraid of confrontation, they push personal responsibility, and they tackle the underlying causes of drug abuse.

The Clinton administration already knows these approaches are working. NIDA recently completed a study of 10,010 drug abusers who entered nearly 100 different treatment programs in 11 cities. Researchers looked at daily drug use a year before and a year after treatment. Long-term residential settings—those with stringent anti-drug policies—did best: Heroin use dropped by 71 percent, cocaine use by 68 percent, and illegal activity in general by 62 percent.

NEP supporters are right to point out that these approaches are often expen-sive and cannot reach most of the nation's estimated 1.2 million IV drug users. Syringe exchanges, they say, are a cost-effective alternative.

NEPs may be cheaper to run, but they are no alternative; they offer no remedy for the ravages of drug addiction. The expense of long-term residential care surely cannot be greater than the social and economic costs of failing to liberate large populations from drug abuse. . . .

Meanwhile, activists decry a lack of drug paraphernalia for eager clients. They call the decision to withhold federal funding "immoral." They want NEPs massively expanded, some demanding no limits on distribution. Says one spokesman, "The one-to-one rule in needle exchange isn't at all connected to reality." New York's ADAPT program gives out at least 350,000 needles a year. "But to meet the demand," says Fatt, "we'd need to give out a million a day."

A million a day? Now that would be a Brave New World: Intravenous drug users with lots of drugs, all the needles they want, and police-free zones in which to network. Are we really to believe this strategy will contain the AIDS virus?

This is not compassion, it is ill-conceived public policy. This is not "saving lives," but abandoning them—consigning countless thousands to drug-induced death on the installment plan. For when a culture winks at drug use, it gets a population of Walters: "Don't get the idea in your mind you're going to control it."

Chapter 4

Should Public Health Measures Be Used to Prevent the Spread of HIV?

CURRENT CONTROVERSIES

Chapter Preface

Thirty-two states have registries that track the number of people with HIV. States use these registries to learn the extent of the epidemic and how to best allocate resources for its prevention and treatment. Of those states, all except Maryland place full names in their registry. In Maryland, a unique identifier (UI)—an alphanumeric code that is based on the patient's Social Security number, date of birth, gender, and race—is used instead of a name. While advocates of civil liberties have lauded Maryland's approach, other organizations question the effectiveness of UI systems.

According to the American Civil Liberties Union (ACLU), name reporting can discourage AIDS testing. In an October 1997 report, the ACLU notes: "One study found that over 60% of individuals tested anonymously would not have tested if their names were reported to public health officials." Under the Maryland system, the UIs for people who test positive for HIV or for CD4 (a type of white blood cell) counts of less than 200 are matched against the UIs in Maryland's AIDS registry. Unmatched CD4 test results are investigated as possible new AIDS cases. The HIV positive test results that have complete UI numbers are matched with the AIDS registry and with prior HIV cases to produce a list of HIV cases that have not yet turned into AIDS. A report issued by the ACLU in December 1997 contends that the UI system has been largely effective and indicates that "UIs must be considered as a viable alternative to names-based reporting."

Not everyone agrees with Maryland's method. Researchers at the Centers for Disease Control and Prevention have expressed concern that the UI system provides incomplete information and does not wholly eliminate confidentiality concerns. UI numbers are often incomplete because certain information, usually the Social Security number, is unavailable. Cynthia David, an assistant professor at the Charles R. Drew University of Medicine and Science in Los Angeles, has noted another problem with the reliance on Social Security numbers. In testimony she gave before the House Subcommittee on Health and Environment, David said: "In some high incidence states such as California, Texas and New York, use of social security numbers as part of a unique identifier system would lead to an underestimation of HIV infected persons in certain demographic groups, such as immigrants."

As the controversy over HIV registries shows, the public health issues of treating and preventing HIV and AIDS often conflict with the right to privacy and other civil liberties. In the following chapter, the authors consider how all those concerns can best be addressed.

Concerns for Civil Rights Have Hobbled Efforts to Control AIDS

by Chandler Burr

About the author: *Chandler Burr is a journalist and contributing editor to* U.S. News & World Report.

Dr. Tom Coburn, a low-key 50-year-old family general practitioner who practices obstetrics, mostly for Medicaid patients, in Muskogee, Oklahoma, is the front-runner for the title of Gay Activists' Public Enemy Number One. It is a designation he is happy to contend for.

In his other job as a Republican congressman ("not my profession, I'm a doctor"), Coburn is the author and primary sponsor of HR-1062, The AIDS Prevention Act of 1997. All the major liberal, civil-liberties, gay, and AIDS organizations—the American Civil Liberties Union (ACLU), the Gay and Lesbian Medical Association, National Organization for Women (NOW), the AIDS Action Council, Gay Men's Health Crisis, People for the American Way, and so on—are in full assault mode against the bill, which if enacted would do something to the AIDS epidemic we've never done before: apply to it the standard public-health disease-containment measures of routine testing of at-risk individuals (although individuals should have the right to refuse testing), confidential reporting by name of those infected to local health authorities, and aggressive partner notification. In other words, it will make public-health personnel treat AIDS—the number one killer of Americans aged 25 to 44—like any other infectious disease.

AIDS, in partial fulfillment of its own championship in the annals of epidemiology (winner, "Most Politicized Disease in the History of the Whole World"), has never been attacked with these measures. Why? Because of a judgment call about who would get hurt. When AIDS weighed in in full force in the mid 1980s, the gay community decided that the disease hurt homosexuals vulnerable to a hostile society at least as much by pitilessly outing them as it did by killing them. Standard public health is about identifying the infected in order to prevent further transmission, but with AIDS, identification was the problem. The gay community, with the best of intentions, believed that the messy, complex, often desperate job of protecting the public health against contagion could be made nice and not hurt anyone.

AIDS in Cuba

This decision produced a rather astounding display of political power. After intense lobbying on the part of gay organizations, state and local public-health officials ultimately with the avid support of the mighty Centers for Disease Control (CDC), made AIDS the first epidemic treated as a civil-rights issue and a threat to individual privacy. All sorts of violations were presented: people with AIDS being expelled from their homes, losing their jobs, being dropped by their insurers. But the greatest threat was that the government would use the virus as an excuse to conduct a new holocaust. This was an explicit and constant warning by the gay and civil-liberties organizations—and they told us there was a country that actually did it: Cuba. Cuba set up concentration camps. Juanita Darling in the *Los Angeles Times* of July 24 recounted in a (relatively) moderate tone what these organizations have been saying for years: "Cuba has been notorious for its draconian treatment of people infected with the virus that causes

> *"After intense lobbying on the part of gay organizations, state and local public-health officials . . . made AIDS the first epidemic treated as a civil-rights issue."*

AIDS: The government has rounded up everyone infected with the human immunodeficiency virus and locked them in sanitariums until they developed AIDS and died." The Cubans, we were told, used traditional epidemiology—testing, reporting, and notification—to track down and persecute homosexuals, and were we to use these measures in the U.S., they would surely be deployed in the same way. So we did not.

What we did instead was use sex education, condoms, and needle exchange, essentially asking people to learn how HIV is transmitted and then to be careful. Columbia University's Ron Bayer created a name for this brand new civil-rights-centered public health—"AIDS exceptionalism"—and in the U.S. all efforts to combat this epidemic have thus been made to pass a high-minded-sounding test: they must not hurt the civil liberties or personal fortunes of the infected. The practice of epidemiology, created by John Snow in the London cholera epidemic of the mid 1880s and used since then to combat tuberculosis, polio, syphilis and gonorrhea, influenza, and on and on, has in the case of AIDS been fundamentally altered.

Rep. Coburn with his bill is demanding a re-examination of the way our country has responded to this public-health crisis. He is doing this in a forward-looking way: HR-1062 aims to get AIDS treated from now on like other diseases from tuberculosis (TB) to hepatitis A. But what makes HR-1062 so controversial is its retrospective aspect. It calls the past silently but inescapably into question.

"Public Health Works"

At 9:00 A.M. on March 13, 1997, at the press conference introducing the bill, Rep. Coburn stepped up to the lectern in the Rayburn House Office Building, looked at the reporters (in the seats), his allies (behind him), and AIDS organizations' spokesmen (grimly lining the walls like prison guards anticipating a riot), and began, "I am convinced that a hundred thousand deaths could have been averted if we had adopted these basic public-health measures in the first place." Expand this statement and it reads: Tom Coburn believes that at least a hundred thousand people, mostly gay men, who should be alive today are dead because certain people, again mostly gay men, with the best of intentions, used their political power to suspend disease-control measures for AIDS.

This is why HR-1062 is, although Coburn has never put it this way, much more than just another bill: it is an accusation. It is the epidemiological equivalent of a class-action lawsuit, an assertion that gay leaders, abetted by their liberal allies, committed mass manslaughter by instituting policies which ensured that in this medical conflagration a virus would use their own people as kindling.

Coburn's is an observation increasingly echoed by the medical establishment. On a national radio show a few weeks after Coburn's press conference, Dr. Frank Judson of Denver's Public Health Department stated: "I have no doubt that lots of people have become infected and lost their lives as a result of these irrational policies we've chosen to follow." Which lends credence to statements of Rep. Coburn's such as: "Public health works, and the people who have died of this disease should have been provided it."

But wait. There's more. Arguably worse than slaughtering your own is slaughtering others. The rate at which people are becoming infected with AIDS is thought to be slowing down

> *"At least a hundred thousand people . . . who should be alive today are dead because certain people . . . used their political power to suspend disease-control measures for AIDS."*

only within one demographic group: gay men. Coburn points out that it is growing, at a rather astounding rate, among blacks, Hispanics, and women, most especially women who have sexual relations with intravenous drug users. If Dr. Coburn is correct in saying that "the new public health" took gay lives, then gay men demanding that these same policies be applied to others at risk is both breathtakingly nearsighted and breathtakingly irresponsible. The political repercussions are chilling. What, to take a for-instance, would happen if the black community were to decide one day that traditional epidemiology would have prevented the transmission of HIV to tens if not hundreds of thousands of black people? Or that the problem of skyrocketing rates of HIV infection among blacks could have been averted but was not owing to gays' blind, dogmatic adherence to self-interest?

Dr. Coburn's accusation is only as solid as the data on which it rests. And here is where things get odd. There are, in fact, excellent data. They come from a country which has bent over backward to care for its citizens infected with HIV, probably spending more on AIDS in proportion to its gross national product than any other nation. It has also instituted a traditional epidemiological regimen against AIDS. It has the most successful AIDS-containment policy of any country in the world. The country is the same one accused of carrying out a holocaust against AIDS sufferers: Cuba.

AIDS Containment in Cuba

The first AIDS case in Cuba surfaced in 1985. If AIDS began as a gay disease in the United States, in Cuba it first turned up in heterosexual soldiers back from their country's military exploits in Africa; that 1985 case was a soldier returning from Mozambique. In Africa, anal intercourse, the most efficient way of spreading the virus, is a quite common means of preserving technical virginity in girls. The rate of sexually transmitted diseases (STDs), which also greatly facilitate transmission, is also extremely high. The sanitariums, in Cuba, were built by the army for the country's returning heroes; persecution of homosexuals had nothing to do with it. In fact, when the disease spread to homosexuals, the sanitariums were among the few places where gay couples were allowed to live together openly. Furthermore, the sanitariums provided and provide the best medical care available in Cuba, 3,500 calories a day, and AIDS-prevention information, not to mention ice cream and air conditioning. Since around 1989, AIDS sufferers have in general been able to choose whether to stay in a sanitarium or live at home, and it has often been difficult to get people to leave.

In any case, as tools for combatting AIDS, the sanitariums are of secondary importance. The real story is the public-health policy Cuba put in place. And this was fiercely and completely traditional. Dr. Jorge Perez, the head of the Pedro Kouri Institute for Tropical and Infectious Diseases and the architect of Cuba's anti-AIDS plan, told me recently in Havana, "From the beginning we treated AIDS like an STD." This meant testing, reporting, and partner notification. "I as a doctor don't have to have someone's permission to test them," said Perez. "I don't ask. Testing isn't mandatory, but I simply prescribe a test when I have good reason." In most of the United States, this is illegal when the test is for HIV.

> *"[Cuba] has the most successful AIDS-containment policy of any country in the world."*

"We have a very active screening program," said Dr. Rigoberto Torres, "testing risk groups, pregnant women, inmates." Again, these practices, which are standard public-health procedures, have been almost entirely blocked in the U.S. by ACLU lawsuits and AIDS political activism, as has contact tracing, which is acknowledged as the most efficient, cost-effective way of identifying infections in subgroups of populations. Studies in the U.S. have shown that partner notification finds more infected people than any other method, and it finds them earlier, when their T-cell count is higher and their prognosis is better.

> *"Studies in the U.S. have shown that partner notification finds more infected people than any other method, and it finds them earlier, when . . . their prognosis is better."*

For the most part, however, we Americans don't notify, or we don't notify effectively, simply because it might "invade people's privacy"—a privacy that has already been invaded by a deadly although treatable virus. Of testing, reporting, and notification Perez says, "These three things are the key of the Cuban [traditionalist] program. We have now done 2 million tests in a population of 11 million, and virtually all sexually active people have been tested. The main source of infected people we get is through contact tracing, about 50 to 60 per cent."

A Successful Strategy

The results of Cuba's program speak for themselves. In 1997, 45,000 people out of the 260-million American population will become infected with the AIDS virus, and so far over 362,000 Americans have died; Cuba, with an 11-million population, has since the start of the epidemic seen 1,681 infected. So far, 442 have died. Control for the population difference, and here is what you get: There have been 35 times more AIDS deaths per capita in the United States than in Cuba. (Of all Americans alive since the start of the epidemic, AIDS has killed 0.14 per cent of them; in Cuba, it has killed 0.004 per cent.)

Compare Cuba to New York City, with its population of around 7.5 million: An estimated 128,700 New Yorkers live with AIDS or HIV, and 63,789 have died. Is very urban New York an unfair comparison? Take Ohio, a Midwestern, predominantly rural state with a population almost exactly the same size as Cuba's: an estimated 10,000 to 18,000 people are HIV positive (this is only an estimate because Ohio doesn't permit HIV reporting), and there have been 9,238 cases of AIDS. Illinois, also Cuba's size, estimates that 30,000 of its citizens are currently HIV-infected (Cuba: 1,239). It has had 19,507 AIDS cases (Cuba: 1,681) and counting.

Look at it another way: In 1993 (the last year for which there are figures) the World Health Organization reported that the U.S. had 276 annual new cases of AIDS per million people. Puerto Rico, another Caribbean island but with one-third Cuba's population, had 654. Brazil was at 75.4, Mexico at 46, and Argentina at 48 per million.

Cuba was at 7. And Cuba's pediatric AIDS system cares for a total of 5 children, whereas Pennsylvania, with the same population, has 122. In the U.S. in 1996, there were 678 pediatric AIDS cases reported to the CDC, which means that our per-capita figure for children with AIDS is 6.5 times higher than Cuba's.

The figures are neither a statistical trick nor Castroite propaganda. (Castro had nothing to do with Cuba's AIDS program, by the way; it is people like Perez, Torres, and Manuel Santine, Cuba's chief epidemiologist, who created and run it.) Cuba's health-care standards are approximately equal to ours; its infant-mortality rate, a good overall indicator, is 11 deaths per 1,000 live births, near the 7 figure of the U.S., United Kingdom, and France. (Canada's is 6. The Dominican Republic's and Mexico's are 35 and 34 respectively.) And one epidemiologist told me of the AIDS stats: "Cuban figures are absolutely reliable and dependable. Surveillance is quite good because they have essentially universal testing and an excellent tracking system. We trust the Cuban figures more than any other country's, where there is underreporting and misdiagnosis,

> *"In the United States, when you go in for a surgical procedure, you get tested for everything, which is just good medicine—but not HIV."*

but, um, don't quote me on that." He meant the United States; the CDC will tell you there could be anywhere from 650,000 to 900,000 Americans infected with HIV; it is the lack of traditional testing that prevents the compilation of a more accurate figure. In Cuba, meanwhile, there are reportedly 1,239 people living with HIV, and the number is probably quite close to exact. If we take the CDC's upper figure (the estimates of some experts are higher) and put it on a per-capita basis, there are around 31 times more HIV-positive Americans than Cubans.

Condoms Are Not a Solution

Besides demonstrating the success traditional methods have against AIDS, the Cuban example also challenges our strategy of throwing condoms at the problem. One American working on AIDS in Cuba told me he had seen "extraordinarily low condom use." Although some condoms of Dutch manufacture are now available, Cuba for years imported Chinese condoms, which were of notoriously low quality—they were actually used by Cubans not in bed but at the market as chits to buy sugar—and yet the infection rate is still dramatically lower than America's. This shouldn't be the case if condoms are the answer and if old-fashioned public health doesn't work.

This is not to say that the Cuban model per se would be right for the United States. It isn't, most specifically the sanitariums. Elinor Burkett, a former AIDS reporter for the *Miami Herald* with extensive experience in Cuba and the author of

The Gravest Show on Earth: America in the Age of AIDS, notes: "What's different in Cuba is that people don't think about individual rights. Most Americans think that when we're balancing social good with individual rights, we err toward the latter. Cubans are trained in the opposite mentality, so my friends in the sanitari-ums . . . believe there's a social good coming out of it." There is also the medical fact that isolation for HIV, a difficult-to-get virus, is unnecessary provided there are 1) testing and notifi-cation to alert those infected and 2) transmission education for them.

> **"The condom solution has failed."**

Nor is it to say that no exceptionalist methods work. On June 27, 1997, the American Medical Association emphatically supported needle exchange, a fa-vorite exceptionalist method that clearly helps reduce HIV transmission. Nor is the exceptionalist Weltanschauung completely wrong. In America, the abundant discrimination visited upon homosexuals and the HIV positive did indeed cre-ate problems for traditional public-health methods. However, the public-health answer is to challenge the discrimination, not eliminate good epidemiology.

Opposition to such epidemiology has, in this country, reached ludicrous pro-portions, actually compromising medical care. Miss Burkett offers her own per-sonal example. "In the United States, when you go in for a surgical procedure, you get tested for everything, which is just good medicine—but not HIV. A few years ago, I had lymphoma. Here is a disease that is 63 times more common among HIV-positive people. I had just been tested and knew I was negative, but my doctors didn't know that. So I go in and I wait for them to suggest I get an HIV test. And I wait and I wait and I wait. And the day I'm starting chemother-apy I ask my doctor why he didn't test me. And he got very defensive. He said, 'Well, I can't test you without your permission, that's the law.' I asked: 'Well, why didn't you suggest it was medically wise?' I knew the answer perfectly well: I was a straight, white, upper-middle-class woman. But it was completely medically irresponsible, because as a doctor you are going to treat my lym-phoma quite differently depending on whether I'm HIV positive or HIV nega-tive. Because of these policies, we are giving heart transplants without routinely testing people. Which is insane. I just don't understand how you're going to practice good medicine without routine testing."

Shifting Political Alignments

From the point of view of HR-1062, what is interesting is that Miss Burkett is echoing the general practitioner from Oklahoma almost word for word. He is a Christian Coalition Republican and she is a devout self-described "old lefty" with numerous gay friends who nevertheless will tell you, "These old [excep-tionalist] policies were born out of a reality which, if it ever existed, certainly doesn't any more."

The Burkett/Coburn symmetry illustrates a subtle shifting of alignments. Dr.

Thomas Coates, Professor of Medicine and Director of the Center for AIDS Prevention Studies at the University of California at San Francisco, is as adept at surviving in the cauldron of left-wing San Francisco AIDS politics as anyone. Dr. Coates recently supported traditionalist measures. His change of heart was prompted by the evidence from AIDS programs abroad: "In the end, the HIV and STD epidemics are unnecessary," he said. "No other industrialized country has these problems. Europe and Australia and New Zealand have gone after these diseases with traditionalist methods and with non-traditionalist, new methods supported by the exceptionalists, and have essentially taken care of them."

The AIDS organizations' resistance to traditionalism is still emphatic, but then cold hard reality is not their strong suit. These are the people who brought you the seductive lie that condoms are the universal answer to all diseases that ride on human sexuality. Gay men have swallowed this, but the condom solution has failed. Coburn contends—and while it is perhaps unprovable it is very interesting—that trust in condoms actually contributed to an increase in transmission of HIV and STDs through increased sexual activity multiplied by the condom breakage rate.

> *"The AIDS community forgets that the ultimate violation of civil rights is being infected with AIDS."*

Moreover—and this should alarm the gay community—despite the current decline in the rate of HIV transmission among gay men, one must note that statistically we are still, as Michael Fumento put it, "the rats [carrying the] fleas of the new plague." Given human nature, today's decline and the desire to believe that the epidemic has been "conquered," accompanied by the inevitable slipping back into unsafe sex and renewed promiscuity, may mean our regaining plague leadership in the future. Gabriel Rotello, a *Newsday* columnist and a gay man who has bucked AIDS dogma, noted recently in his book *Sexual Ecology* that the backlash has already begun. "Editorial boards . . . have moved to distance themselves from gay-run AIDS groups they once unquestioningly supported. Liberal politicians have begun asking tough questions in private while becoming noncommittal in public. Friends of gay people have begun to wonder aloud at the high rates of unsafe sex and transmission."

A Difficult Problem

In the end, the public-health response to AIDS is not an easy problem. Do we, by implementing effective policies, hurt the small number of individuals who will, inevitably, be outed and risk being fired from jobs, and thereby save many times their number from exposure to a devastating virus? Or do we hurt a large number of individuals by refusing to implement policies to combat the disease that will poison their bodies? One of Dr. Coburn's allies answers the question succinctly: "The AIDS community forgets that the ultimate violation of civil rights is being infected with AIDS." And 35 times more deaths per capita under an exceptionalist regime indicates that, somewhere, something went very, very wrong.

Back on Capitol Hill, Tom Coburn will spend the fall of 1997 working hard on his bill. It aims to chart a new course on AIDS policy, but it is a very delicate matter when under the old course thousands of people have already died and thousands more are sick and the figures seem all out of proportion and you have this nagging little question of responsibility. Dr. Coburn might prefer not to get into it at all (it could certainly complicate the debate), but the fact is, and he knows it, that the mere existence of his bill is forcing an entire political community to step up and calmly respond to the accusation of mass manslaughter. They are not particularly calm at the moment. But you would be hysterical, too, if someone said to you, "Through everything you've worked for, by everything you believe, and with everything you've fought to maintain, you have helped to kill a hundred thousand human beings."

HIV Testing of Pregnant Women and Newborns Should Be Mandatory

by Netty Mayersohn, interviewed by Cory Ser Vaas

About the author: *Netty Mayersohn is an assemblywoman from New York. Cory Ser Vaas is editor-in-chief of the* Saturday Evening Post.

"It was the Tuskegee experiment all over again [from 1932–1972, the U.S. government conducted an experiment in which they withheld treatment from a group of African American men who were suffering from syphilis in order to track progression of the disease]," says Netty Mayersohn. The veteran New York assemblywoman was appalled when she discovered that New York hospitals were testing newborns for HIV but not informing the parents and doctors so that the babies could be treated. She "put her life on hold" for three years to pass legislation that would mandate HIV testing and reporting for newborns in New York State. The program initiated by her "Baby AIDS" bill became the first of its kind in the nation.

We reached Assemblywoman Mayersohn at her district office in Flushing, New York, to ask her about her landmark AIDS legislation.

Cory Ser Vaas: *When did you first become interested in the plight of babies infected with HIV?*

Netty Mayersohn: Four years ago I had a meeting with the state medical society. They told me that every baby in New York State was being tested for HIV antibodies, but that no one—not the parents, not the doctor—was allowed to be notified when a baby tested positive. This was done because the Centers for Disease Control and Prevention (CDC) were conducting a blind testing program in 44 states in order to track the epidemic to see where they had to place resources. But confidentiality had to be the policy. They started doing these tests in 1987. Six or seven years later in New York State alone, we were seeing something like 1,800 babies each year testing positive [for HIV]. I was reading in the medical journals that they weren't getting to the babies early enough to prevent pneumocystis pneumonia. The babies were coming in too late, and because no one was being notified that these babies were at risk, they were dying of opportunistic infections, infections that could have been prevented. In my conversations with the CDC, I asked, "At what point do we stop testing for the purpose of statistics and use it to give people the information they need to have to save lives?"

The Baby AIDS Bill

So you introduced the Baby AIDS bill.

I introduced legislation in March of '93 stating that when babies tested positive for HIV, mothers had to be informed so we could get the kids into treatment. I put everything else aside. I really put my life on hold for the three years it took to get the bill passed.

You have to understand, of the 1,800 babies that tested positive each year in New York State alone, 75 percent were not really HIV infected. They had their mothers' antibodies, which their own bodies shake off over a period of time—about 12 to 14 months. But it did mean in every case that the mother was infected, and if she wasn't warned that the virus can be transmitted through breast-feeding, then we were allowing healthy babies to become infected.

I was just so astounded. This was the Tuskegee experiment all over again.

What was the reaction to the Baby AIDS legislation?

The opposition was formidable—the League of Women Voters, the American Civil Liberties Union (ACLU), Gay Men's Health Crisis, the American Red Cross, the March of Dimes all opposed the bill.

Organizations you would think would have no connection to groups that insisted on privacy over public health, but there's a network among many of these groups, and together they presented powerful opposition.

All of these groups should have supported the legislation. Shouldn't the Gay Men's Health Crisis have been supportive? They could see the devastation! Shouldn't the women's groups have been supportive? We're talking about infants, newborns. At any rate, out of 150 assembly members, I had 94 sponsors for the bill. Every newspaper in New York State from the major newspapers to the locals was supporting the legislation. There was general outrage, yet it took me three years because AIDS activists and the

> *"'At what point do we stop testing for the purpose of statistics and use it to give people the information they need to have to save lives?'"*

gay community in certain parts of the city had a great deal of political clout. They were able to hold up the bill for three years. It was the legislature and Governor George Pataki's strong support for the bill that made the difference. We were able to pass it finally in June of '96. It was just an incredible issue. I still don't understand the opposition, and I've heard all the arguments.

Mandatory Testing vs. Voluntary Testing

What were some of the arguments against?

AIDS activists and civil rights groups presented the most incredible arguments against changing the law to allow mothers to know the test results. For example, if the baby tested positive, it meant the mother had AIDS, and giving her the information was a violation of confidentiality and her right "not to know" about her own condition. That is hardly a public health argument. And can you imagine any caring mother not wanting to know everything about her baby's condition? The fact is, she will find out eventually. We wanted her to have the information before she came back to the hospital six months later with an infant dying of preventable pneumocystis pneumonia.

> *"In every case that the mother was infected . . . we were allowing healthy babies to become infected."*

Then there was the argument that it was more important to persuade women to be tested voluntarily during pregnancy than to test the infant at birth. This, they said, would give the mother the opportunity to get AZT, which has been shown to reduce transmission if treatment is started during the prenatal period. But they presented it as an "either-or" choice, which of course it is not. While we can all agree that women should be counseled and persuaded to be tested during pregnancy, this has nothing to do with the right of the infant to medical treatment at birth—even the infant whose mother may be a drug addict in denial, who does not access prenatal care. In addition, because mothers are aware that the babies will be tested at birth, we are able to persuade more mothers to be tested during pregnancy.

The opposition never understood that women cannot afford the luxury of avoiding bad news. Women must know their medical condition so that they can make important healthcare decisions for themselves and their babies; they must know so that they can avoid spreading the disease to others; they must know so that they can make decisions on future pregnancies; and they must know so that they can make arrangements for the care of their children when they, themselves, can no longer care for them.

I kept looking, frankly, for that one logical argument that would help me understand the opposition, but I never found it. There was no rationale. It was all driven by emotion, the fear of discrimination. My response to that was we'll deal with discrimination. In fact, we have.

Under the Americans with Disabilities Act, we're dealing with all kinds of discrimination, and the courts have been very supportive. Where there is evidence of discrimination, courts have ruled in favor of the complainant. But this does not mean that we can ignore what is happening in the whole area of public health in dealing with HIV and AIDS. You know, we announced a major victory because we reduced the incidence of tuberculosis in New York City, but we did it by using very strong public-health strategies.

We said, if you are infected, the health department has the right to go into your home, test every member of your family. If health officials feel you are not taking your medication, they can put you into a detention center to make sure that you do take your medication. This is considered good public-health strategy, and we have, in fact, gotten a handle on tuberculosis. The same rules have been applied to every other infectious disease. Syphilis, for awhile, was almost extinct because of the public-health measures that we had taken. But with this disease [AIDS], they are not allowing us to do the kinds of things we should be doing to stop the spread of the epidemic. It's truly beyond comprehension. . . .

Federal Legislation

But the Baby AIDS bill broke the ice.

Yes, the first breakthrough was the Baby AIDS bill. What it did more than anything was open up the debate. Doctors suddenly were not afraid to come out and say, yes, this is something we should be doing. Before, it was like the story of the emperor who had no clothes. No one wanted to admit the policy was wrong. There must have been 50 organizations opposing notification. It was as if doctors were fearful about coming forward. In fact, so many doctors came to me and said privately, "I agree with what you are doing, but I can't say it." Many of the grants doctors get in the hospitals they work for go for counseling programs which have to be approved by some of the opposition groups. So there was a reluctance to get anybody to step forward, but now they're doing it.

> *"Women cannot afford the luxury of avoiding bad news."*

Did you have support for your bill from hemophiliac groups?

No. And what happened to hemophiliacs was horrible. At the very beginning of the epidemic, when they knew there was something wrong with the blood supply, they couldn't screen blood donors. As a result, half the hemophiliac population was wiped out. One day we're going to look back at this whole period and recognize the insanity. We could have prevented so many deaths and so much tragedy, yet the very people who should have been most interested in stopping the epidemic were the people who fought hardest for the principle of privacy over public health. . . .

Successful Results

What results have you seen in New York from the passage of the Baby AIDS bill?

When I first discovered the issue, we had counseling programs in 24 of the hospitals where high-risk women gave birth. The purpose was to convince women to be tested. The success rate was incredibly bad. About 17 percent of the women agreed to be tested. Twenty-four percent knew their results when they came into the hospital because they had been tested, or as a result of previous pregnancies. Almost 60 percent of the infants were going home without anyone knowing that they had tested positive. Since we started the [mandatory] newborn testing, we're getting 100 percent of the infants identified. The latest health department statistics show that 98.8 percent of infants and their mothers are being directed into treatment; something like 1.2 percent had, for some reason, disappeared. They either went out of state or whatever. It's still part of the record. We know who the babies are, and if they ever show up, we'll be able to get them into treatment. The success rate is phenomenal. . . .

> *"The very people who should have been most interested in stopping the epidemic were the people who fought hardest for the principle of privacy over public health."*

Now that you have achieved your goal with the Baby AIDS bill, what are you working on?

I'm working on the partner-notification bill. That was my first battle, but I dropped it for the babies. I knew the babies were something that people would understand and that babies would raise public awareness of how we deal with AIDS. Partner notification I realized would be more difficult. Nevertheless, we can no longer buy into the arguments that HIV will go underground if we apply traditional public health measures to curb the epidemic. The reality today is that there is treatment available and HIV-infected people are seeking medical care. This gives us the opportunity to do aggressive contact tracing so that we can prevent the spread of the epidemic to uninfected people who are at great risk because they don't have a clue that their partner is HIV infected. HIV is a slow-moving virus and there can be a significant lapse of time before transmission. The time has come for us to show real compassion by not allowing another human being to be unnecessarily exposed to this deadly virus.

Public Health Measures Have Not Been Proven to Prevent the Spread of AIDS

by Gabriel Rotello

About the author: *Gabriel Rotello is the author of* Sexual Ecology: AIDS and the Destiny of Gay Men.

In 1936, Thomas Parran, the director of the nation's anti-venereal-disease program, told a conference of medical professionals, "Every case must be located, reported, its source ascertained and all contacts then informed about the possibility of infection and if infected, treated."

And so it has been ever since for sexually transmitted diseases. Except for AIDS. And for good reason.

During epidemics of most sexually transmitted diseases, state public health authorities routinely test large numbers of people, sometimes without their knowledge, report names of the afflicted to health departments and try to trace and inform their sexual partners. The main goal is to identify people who do not know they are infected and get them into treatment as quickly as possible, before they can infect others.

AIDS has always been largely exempted from these traditional methods of managing public health. But now a major new debate is questioning "AIDS exceptionalism." And surprisingly, many of those questioning it are AIDS advocates themselves, the very folks who once drew a bright line between AIDS and other sexually transmitted diseases.

But there is reason to be cautious before we jettison laws or health policies that insure confidentiality for people infected with H.I.V.

The AIDS Exception

For years, AIDS seemed to render traditional approaches to containing outbreaks of venereal disease not only useless, but also counterproductive. Useless

Reprinted from Gabriel Rotello, "AIDS Is Still an Exceptional Disease," *The New York Times*, August 27, 1997. Reprinted with permission from *The New York Times*.

because there were no effective treatments, so identifying victims was likely to produce despair rather than action. Counterproductive because society's stigmatization of gay men and intravenous drug users, the two populations most affected by AIDS, made these groups justifiably wary of anything that might expose them to further discrimination.

AIDS advocates feared that reporting the names of those with H.I.V. and contacting their sexual partners could easily lead to exposure and discrimination. Some even feared a slippery slope leading to eventual quarantine and criminalization of the H.I.V. positive.

It didn't help that many of those calling for traditional approaches in the 1980's were openly hostile to gay men and people with AIDS. As public health authorities quickly learned in dealing with the politically mobilized gay community, effective prevention is impossible if you drive the people most at risk away from the health care system.

Finally, it was argued that in populations with large numbers of sexual partners, contact tracing would be both very expensive and largely useless, since it requires individuals to remember everyone they had sex with.

It seemed far wiser to spend what little prevention money was available—and it has never been enough—on trying to get high-risk populations to alter behavior by emphasizing that everyone was at potential risk.

No Proof

Now, however, new treatments are vastly improving and extending the lives of many people with H.I.V., although the rate of new infections remains high. Studies indicate that the earlier people enter therapy, the better the prognosis. If AIDS is no longer uniquely fatal and untreatable, advocates ask, should we keep treating it that way? Shouldn't we go back to the tried and true methods of the past?

Well, maybe, but not so fast. The new debate indicates a pragmatic desire to embrace whatever might work, and that's great. But it also holds potential dangers. The old methods were certainly tried, but were they necessarily true?

The fact is that practices like name reporting and contact tracing arose in the late 19th and early 20th centuries, before there was any scientific way of determining whether they worked. They may have satisfied a popular demand that health authorities do something, but the fact is, we don't really know how effective they were.

> *"There is reason to be cautious before we jettison laws or health policies that insure confidentiality for people infected with H.I.V."*

Contact tracing may have made a dent in rates of transmission, but epidemics of syphilis, gonorrhea, chlamydia and other sexually transmitted diseases raged on anyway.

Even some who advocate name reporting and contact tracing for people with

H.I.V., like Marcia Angell, executive editor of the *New England Journal of Medicine*, acknowledge that evidence is lacking.

"Nobody can document or prove that traditional methods of control would work better at containing AIDS," Dr. Angell recently told the *Atlantic Monthly*, "because nobody has done what would be necessary to get such proof." Namely, studying two populations in which different methods were tried.

Even today, there is a long list of basic questions we do not have answers to—What makes some people practice safer sex? What encourages some people to enter the health care system? What drives others away? Does knowing whether you are infected affect your sexual behavior?

AIDS Bashing Still Exists

And there is still a lot of AIDS bashing out there. A new [1997] bill in Congress, sponsored by Representative Tom Coburn, Republican of Oklahoma, calls for a national registry of all H.I.V.-positive people (there is no such registry for any other disease), authorizes health professionals to refuse to perform invasive procedures until a patient has been tested for H.I.V., and allows funeral homes to refuse to perform procedures unless the deceased has been tested.

It ignores needle exchange, a technique that has now been scientifically proved to prevent H.I.V. transmission without increasing drug use. And shockingly, the bill provides not a

> *"'Nobody can document or prove that traditional methods of control would work better at containing AIDS.'"*

penny in additional money, even though its provisions have been estimated to cost hundreds of millions of dollars per year.

Thankfully, most Congressional observers doubt that this punitive bill will pass. But it vividly illustrates the fact that authoritarian, anti-scientific attitudes about H.I.V. prevention are still powerful.

This is not to say that civil liberties are absolutes when it comes to dire threats to the public health. The rights of infected people must be balanced against the right of all people to protect themselves. If traditional methods can be shown to prevent new infections and bring treatment to the infected, they should be considered.

But the key is whether these methods can be shown to be effective.

To do that, health authorities have an obligation to apply scientific rigor to their own methods and assumptions. And society has an obligation to insure that whatever methods are approved, they strive to balance civil liberties with public safety, encourage people to enter the health system rather than drive them away, and provide adequate financing and care to the afflicted.

The debate on AIDS exceptionalism is a healthy sign that AIDS advocates are open to new ideas. But it should proceed with caution, and with a healthy sense of what we still don't know, and what we need to find out.

Mandatory HIV Testing of Pregnant Women and Newborns Is Unconstitutional

by the American Civil Liberties Union

About the author: *The American Civil Liberties Union is a national organization that works to defend civil rights and liberties guaranteed by law and the U.S. Constitution.*

The American Civil Liberties Union opposes mandatory, non-consensual HIV testing of pregnant women and newborns. We all have the right, protected by the Constitution, to be free of unnecessary government control. To take any compulsory medical action—such as forced HIV testing—the government must prove that there is no less intrusive means of achieving its goal of promoting public health. In the case of pregnant women and newborns, the facts do not justify mandatory HIV testing but rather show that counseling and voluntary testing is a less intrusive way of promoting health. Indeed, counseling and voluntary testing are more effective than forced testing because they encourage women to receive ongoing medical care for themselves and their babies, instead of driving them away from health care services. The Centers for Disease Control and Prevention (CDC), the government's own medical experts, have recommended counseling and voluntary testing, as opposed to mandatory testing. Opponents of testing without consent also include the American Academy of Pediatrics (AAP), the American College of Obstetrics & Gynecology (ACOG) and the March of Dimes.

CDC HIV-Testing of Newborns

The CDC currently tests unidentified blood samples of newborns in order to better understand the nature and extent of HIV in this country. Because the

Reprinted from "ACLU Position Statement on Prenatal and Newborn HIV Testing," available at www.aclu.org/congress/prenatal.html. Reprinted with permission from the American Civil Liberties Union.

CDC testing is done not for the purpose of diagnosis but for statistical tracking, the samples are not name-labelled, nor are they collected or tested in the manner in which a sample would be if it were to be tested for diagnostic purposes. The CDC's mission is not to provide diagnostic laboratory testing, and the CDC may very well consider a testing program that had to be redesigned to accommodate diagnostic as well as epidemiological uses to be excessively compromised. Thus, "unblinding" of the CDC study could result in no universal newborn HIV screening for any purpose.

Newborn Testing Cannot Prevent Prenatal HIV Transmission

The results of HIV tests of newborns indicate not whether the newborn is HIV-infected, but whether maternal HIV antibodies are present. If a newborn tests positive, we learn that the mother has HIV and that the odds are roughly one in four that the infant itself is HIV positive. Unfortunately, there is no post-birth treatment at this time to reduce these odds—AZT or other anti-retroviral drugs do not prevent sero-conversion in the infant. The primary treatment is antibiotics administered prophylactically several times a day to ward off pneumocystis pneumonia (an AIDS-induced pneumonia that is particularly virulent in infants) and to wait for a period of several weeks, after which it is possible to determine an infant's own HIV status by further laboratory tests.

However, before and during birth, steps can be taken to reduce the risk of maternal-infant transmission. One study suggests that AZT given after the fourteenth week of pregnancy, continued during delivery and given to the new infant for the first six weeks of life can reduce the risk of infection to the infant by as much as two-thirds, from approximately 25 percent (one in four) to 8 percent (one in twelve).

Any opportunity for prevention of in utero HIV infection makes bringing women into prenatal care crucial. Not only does prenatal care decrease the risk of prematurity with its markedly increased mortality, it also provides the opportunity for the woman to learn about her HIV status and the benefits and risks of AZT treatment as a prevention for infecting her infant. Additionally, knowledge of maternal HIV status before birth makes possible a decision to deliver by caesarian section, which is believed to further reduce the risk of infecting the infant.

> *"In the case of pregnant women and newborns, the facts do not justify mandatory HIV testing."*

Another reason for early detection of HIV infection in pregnancy is to advise the infected mother not to breast-feed. Although this has not been a major problem in the United States because so few women at higher risk of HIV infection breast-feed, proponents of mandatory HIV testing of newborns cite protection against infection from breast-feeding as one of the benefits of such testing. They ignore the critical fact that breast-feeding must begin shortly after birth, several days before existing tests can be completed to determine the presence of maternal HIV antibodies. In fact, colostrum, the breast secretion during the first early days after birth, may pose a greater threat of infection to the infant than milk produced thereafter. These facts provide further support for the importance of prenatal care, including counseling and voluntary testing, as opposed to mandatory newborn testing.

Voluntary Testing Is More Effective than Mandatory Testing

As the CDC has recently confirmed, counseling and voluntary testing of pregnant women for HIV is more effective than mandatory testing. Mandatory testing of pregnant women and newborns would have detrimental public health consequences, most significantly by deterring women, especially low income women, from seeking prenatal care at all. Whenever mandatory testing has been imposed people have been frightened away. For example, during the two years that the state of Illinois required HIV-antibody testing of people seeking marriage licenses, approximately 40,000 people left the state to get married elsewhere.

By frightening women away from health care providers both during and after pregnancy, some HIV-infected children will neither be identified nor treated. Mandatory testing of a recalcitrant patient will accomplish only ascertainment of HIV status—it does not get either the mother or her child into treatment. Any type of effective medical treatment for children requires the participation and cooperation of their caretakers. Proper management of chronic, infectious, incurable disease in a family requires a tremendous amount of effort—and mother and doctor teamwork—over time, particularly when both mother and child are afflicted. Medicines must be given regularly, procedures must be developed and followed, regular doctor's visits are critical. Without trust there is rarely compliance, especially when a woman is confronting not only the possibility that her child has an incurable disease but the certainty that she does as well.

> *"Mandatory testing of pregnant women and newborns would have detrimental public health consequences."*

Discrimination

Another fact which would drive women away from health care providers who forcibly test them or their children is that these women are susceptible to the same kinds of discrimination faced by others if it becomes known that they are infected with HIV. The possible losses of custody of their children, of their jobs, health insurance, apartments, and other harms, including the risk of broader disclosure and dissemination of their HIV status, are all very real concerns. In addition, many African-American and Latina women may fear mandatory testing and the disclosure of the results based on past histories of discrimination and also due to past negative experiences with health care providers.

In other situations where there is undisputed medical value in learning test results, the sensitivity of the issues involved and the nature of the personal decisions they engender has led to a recognition that such tests should be done only when the patient consents. For example, amniocentesis testing for chromosomal abnormalities and hereditary diseases is recommended for pregnant women over age 35— but it is not mandated by law. Screening for Downs' syndrome and sickle cell diseases are treated similarly. While syphilis testing for pregnant women is mandatory, syphilis can be safely and effectively cured and mandatory syphilis testing does not drive women away from health care providers.

> *"Mandatory testing of a recalcitrant patient will accomplish only ascertainment of HIV status—it does not get either the mother or her child into treatment."*

Currently there is no requirement that pregnant women be routinely educated about HIV and possible treatments to reduce the risk of infecting their babies, or given the opportunity to be tested for HIV. Yet such counseling at the beginning of pregnancy makes the most sense in terms of the parent's decision-making ability about health consequences for the child. Routine non-coercive counseling regarding the benefits and burdens of testing and treatment ensures that rational choices are made by the prospective parents at the most appropriate time. Linking testing to the provision of services has been shown to increase the rate of voluntary consent for testing. Experience indicates that under these circumstances most women will probably agree to be tested, and they can then make informed decisions about the use of AZT, antibiotics and other treatments while pregnant or after birth. For example, at Harlem Hospital in New York City, over 90 percent of counseled women consent to testing. Similar proportions have been reported at Johns Hopkins Hospital in Baltimore, Maryland, at Grady Hospital in Atlanta, Georgia and elsewhere. If, after counseling, women do not get tested for HIV, they will have the knowledge to make reasoned choices about breast-feeding, caesarean sections and termination of the pregnancy.

A non-coercive health care environment, ongoing care, and access to services are what will bring women and children to health care services—mandatory HIV testing will drive them away.

Mandatory Testing Is Unconstitutional

Counseling and voluntary HIV testing are a constitutionally required less intrusive alternative to mandatory testing of pregnant women and newborns. Non-consensual testing implicates a broad range of constitutional protections. Pregnant women and mothers of newborns, like everyone else in this country, have the right to decision-making about their own bodies; the right to control over medical information; the right to be free of unreasonable searches and seizures by the government; and the right to direct the course of their medical treatment and the medical treatment of their children. They also have the right to equal protection of the law, which is called into question by testing provisions which single out pregnant women, but not men considering having children, as well as by disproportionately affecting women of color.

When these rights are intruded upon, the Constitution requires that the government act in the least intrusive way that will further its goal. The goal of HIV-testing programs is the promotion of health. Counseling and voluntary testing are far less intrusive measures than mandatory, non-consensual testing, and experience strongly indicates that counseling and voluntary testing will more effectively further the goal of promoting health than forced testing would.

Recommendation

More than a decade into the AIDS epidemic in this country we have learned that the spread of HIV is most effectively controlled by voluntary, rather than coercive, measures. If we are truly concerned with the health of women and children then this principle must not be forgotten. To advance the health of women and children and to comply with the constitutional imperative of least intrusive alternatives, counseling and voluntary testing and treatment programs for pregnant women and newborns should be implemented to encourage them to receive ongoing medical care.

Bibliography

Books

Peter Lewis Allen	*The Wages of Sin: Sex and Disease, Past and Present.* Chicago: University of Chicago Press, 2000.
David I. Bernstein and Lawrence R. Stanberry, eds.	*Sexually Transmitted Diseases: Vaccines, Prevention, and Control.* San Diego: Academic Press, 2000.
Elinor Burkett	*The Gravest Show on Earth: America in the Age of AIDS.* Boston: Houghton Mifflin, 1995.
Peter Duesberg	*Inventing the AIDS Virus.* Washington, DC: Regnery, 1996.
Lawrence O. Gostin and Zita Lazzarini	*Human Rights and Public Health in the AIDS Pandemic.* New York: Oxford University Press, 1997.
Jacob Lipman	*Soap, Water, and Sex: A Lively Guide to the Benefits of Sexual Hygiene and to Coping with Sexually Transmitted Diseases.* Amherst, NY: Prometheus Books, 1998.
Lisa Marr	*Sexually Transmitted Diseases: A Physician Tells You What You Need to Know.* Lanham, MD: Johns Hopkins University Press, 1999.
Joe S. McIlhaney and Marion McIlhaney	*Sex: What You Don't Know Can Kill You.* Grand Rapids, MI: Baker Books, 1997.
Adrian Mindel, ed.	*Condoms.* London: BMJ, 2000.
Susan Moore, Anne Mitchell, and Doreen A. Rosenthal	*Youth, AIDS, and Sexually Transmitted Diseases.* New York: Routledge, 1997.
Jeffrey S. Nevid	*Choices: Sex in the Age of STDs.* Needham Heights, MA: Allyn and Bacon, 1997.
Cindy Patton	*Fatal Advice: How Safe-Sex Education Went Wrong.* Durham, NC: Duke University Press, 1996.
Gabriel Rotello	*Sexual Ecology: AIDS and the Destiny of Gay Men.* New York: Dutton, 1997.
Lawrence R. Stanberry	*Understanding Herpes.* Jackson: University of Mississippi Press, 1998.

Sexually Transmitted Diseases

Samuel G. Woods	*Everything You Need to Know About STD: Sexually Transmitted Disease*. New York: Rosen, 1997.

Periodicals

Shannon Brownlee, Marci McDonald, and Elise Hackerman	"AIDS Comes to Small Town America," *U.S. News & World Report*, November 10, 1997.
Chandler Burr	"The AIDS Exception: Privacy vs. Public Health," *Atlantic Monthly*, June 1997.
Geoffrey Cowley	"Fighting the Disease: What Can Be Done," *Newsweek*, January 17, 2000.
Nina Elder	"Teenagers and Herpes," *Better Homes and Gardens*, October 1999.
Thomas R. Eng	"The Hidden Epidemic," *Issues in Science and Technology*, Summer 1997.
Jon Fuller	"Needle Exchange: Saving Lives," *America*, July 18, 1998.
Jerome E. Groopman	"Contagion," *New Yorker*, September 13, 1999.
Zondra Hughes	"Risky Business: What's Behind the Surge in STDs," *Ebony*, January 2000.
Leslie Laurence	"Special Report: Sexual Health Emergency," *Glamour*, August 1998.
Sara Lippmann	"Transmission Complete: Eight Surprises You Don't Want to Find in Your Bed," *Gentlemen's Quarterly*, November 1999.
Tom Masland	"Breaking the Silence," *Newsweek*, July 17, 2000.
Christina Matera and Melanie Mannarino	"The ABC's of STDs," *Seventeen*, January 1998.
Jodie Morse	"Preaching Chastity in the Classroom," *Time*, October 18, 1999.
The New York Times	"Shifting Demographics of HIV," July 1, 1998.
Peter Piot	"Global AIDS Epidemic: Time to Turn the Tide," *Science*, June 23, 2000.
Michael Specter	"Doctors Powerless as AIDS Rakes Africa," *The New York Times*, August 6, 1998.
Steve Sternberg	"Risky Sex Breeds Neglected Epidemic," *Science News*, November 30, 1996.
Sheryl Gay Stolberg	"U.S. Awakes to Epidemic of Sexual Diseases," *The New York Times*, March 9, 1998.
John Stoltenberg	"Of Microbes and Manhood," *Ms*, August/September 2000.
Anthony Tedesco	"Make Me Wear a Condom," *Mademoiselle*, November 1998.

Organizations to Contact

The editors have compiled the following list of organizations concerned with the issues debated in this book. The descriptions are derived from materials provided by the organizations. All have publications or information available for interested readers. The list was compiled on the date of publication of the present volume; the information provided here may change. Be aware that many organizations take several weeks or longer to respond to inquiries, so allow as much time as possible.

Advocates for Youth
1025 Vermont Ave. NW, Suite 200, Washington, DC 20005
(202) 347-5700 • fax: (202) 347-2263
e-mail: info@advocatesforyouth.org • website: www.advocatesforyouth.org

Advocates for Youth supports programs that increase youths' opportunities and abilities to make healthy decisions about sexuality. It publishes the newsletters *Passages* and *Transitions* as well as fact sheets on STDs and AIDS.

AIDS Coalition to Unleash Power (ACT UP)
332 Bleecker St., G5, New York, NY 10014
(212) 966-4873
e-mail: actupny@panix.com • website: www.actupny.org

ACT UP is a group of individuals committed to direct action to end the AIDS crisis. Through education and demonstrations, ACT UP fights against discrimination and for adequate funding for AIDS research, health care, and housing for people with AIDS. It also supports the dissemination of information about safer sex, clean needles, and other AIDS prevention. ACT UP publishes action manuals, such as *Time to Become an AIDS Activist*, and online action reports.

The Alan Guttmacher Institute
120 Wall St., New York, NY 10005
(212) 248-1111 • fax: (212) 248-1951
e-mail: info@agi-usa.org • website: www.agi-usa.org

The institute works to protect and expand the reproductive choices of all women and men. It strives to ensure people's access to the information and services they need to exercise their rights and responsibilities concerning sexual activity, reproduction, and family planning. Among the institute's publications are the books *Teenage Pregnancy in Industrialized Countries* and *Today's Adolescents, Tomorrow's Parents: A Portrait of the Americas* and the report *Sex and America's Teenagers*.

American Civil Liberties Union (ACLU)
125 Broad St., 18th Floor, New York, NY 10004-2400
(212) 549-2500
e-mail: aclu@aclu.org • website: www.aclu.org

The ACLU is a national organization that works to defend Americans' civil rights guaranteed by the U.S. Constitution. The ACLU's Lesbian and Gay Rights/AIDS Project handles litigation, education, and public policy work on behalf of gays and lesbians. It publishes the semiannual newsletter *Civil Liberties Alert* as well as policy papers such as "AIDS and Civil Liberties."

American Foundation for AIDS Research (AmFAR)
120 Wall St., 13th Floor, New York, NY 10005
(212) 806-1600 • fax: (212) 806-1601
e-mail: webmaster@amfar.org • website: www.amfar.org

AmFAR supports AIDS prevention and research and advocates AIDS-related public policy. It publishes several monographs, compendiums, journals, and periodic publications, including the *AIDS/HIV Treatment Directory*, published twice a year; the newsletter *HIV/AIDS Educator and Reporter*, published three times a year; and the quarterly *AmFAR* newsletter.

American Social Health Association (ASHA)
PO Box 13827, Research Triangle Park, NC 27709
(919) 361-8400 • fax: (919) 361-8425
Herpes hot line: (919) 361-8488
website: www.ashastd.org

ASHA is a nonprofit organization dedicated to stopping sexually transmitted diseases and their harmful consequences. It advocates increased federal funding for STD programs and sound public policies on STD control. The association distributes the quarterly newsletter *STD News* and maintains an online sexual health glossary. Its Herpes Resource Center publishes the quarterly newsletter the *Helper*. ASHA's Women's Health Program provides information on pelvic inflammatory disease, vaginitis, Pap tests, and the effects of herpes simplex and HIV testing on pregnancy.

Center for AIDS Prevention Studies
University of California, San Francisco
74 New Montgomery, Suite 600, San Francisco, CA 94105
(415) 597-9100 • fax: (415) 597-9213
website: www.caps.ucsf.edu

The center is committed to the prevention of HIV and AIDS. It sponsors research on the risk factors for AIDS and publishes a newsletter, fact sheets, and press releases.

Centers for Disease Control and Prevention (CDC) Center for HIV, STD, and TB Prevention (CHSTP)
1600 Clifton Rd. NE, Atlanta, GA 30333
(888) CDC-FACT (232-3228) • fax: (888) CDC-FAXX (232-3299)
National STD hot line: (800) 227-8922
e-mail: NCHSTP@cdc.gov • website: www.cdc.gov/nchstp/od/nchstp.html

The CDC is the government agency charged with protecting the public health of the nation by preventing and controlling diseases and by responding to public health emergencies. The CHSTP, a program of the CDC, publishes fact sheets on STDs and the *HIV/AIDS Prevention Newsletter.*

Citizens Alliance for VD Awareness (CAVDA)
PO Box 31915, Chicago, IL 60631-0915
(847) 398-3378 • fax: (847) 398-7309

CAVDA is a not-for-profit organization that produces informational and educational products for use within the disciplines of STD and AIDS control. The alliance also publishes a quarterly newsletter, *STD Spotlight.*

Family Health International (FHI)
PO Box 13950, Research Triangle Park, NC 27709
(919) 544-7040 • fax: (919) 544-7261
website: www.fhi.org

FHI is a not-for-profit organization committed to helping women and men have access to safe, effective, acceptable, and affordable family planning methods; preventing the spread of AIDS and other sexually transmitted diseases; and improving the health of women and children. Its AIDS Control and Prevention Project publishes an annual report and the book *Control of Sexually Transmitted Diseases: A Handbook for the Design and Management of Programs.*

Health Education AIDS Liaison (HEAL)
PO Box 1103, New York, NY 10113
(212) 873-0780 • fax: (212) 873-0891
e-mail: revdocnyc@aol.com • website: www.healaids.com

HEAL is a nonprofit organization that challenges the HIV=AIDS hypothesis and HIV-based treatment protocols. They are the leading source for comprehensive information on the many effective, nontoxic, natural, and holistic approaches to recovering and maintaining health.

HIV/AIDS Treatment Information Service (ATIS)
PO Box 6303, Rockville, MD 20849-6303
(800) HIV-0440 (448-0440) • fax: (301) 519-6616
e-mail: atis@hivatis.org • website: www.hivatis.org

ATIS provides information about federally approved treatment guidelines for HIV and AIDS. It publishes *Principles of Therapy of HIV Infection* as well as reports and guidelines for treating HIV infection in adults, adolescents, and children.

Kaiser Family Foundation
2400 Sand Hill Rd., Menlo Park, CA 94025
(650) 854-9400 • fax: (650) 854-4800
website: www.kff.org

The foundation is an independent health care philanthropy concerned with reproductive health and the spread of STDs. It publishes the reports *Sex Education in the Schools, The Demography of Sexual Behavior, 1997 National Survey of Americans on AIDS/HIV*, and daily online health reports.

Medical Institute for Sexual Health
PO Box 162306, Austin, TX 78716-2306
(512) 328-6268 • fax: (512) 328-6269
e-mail: medinstitute@medinstitute.org • website: www.medinstitute.org

The Medical Institute for Sexual Health is a nonprofit organization dedicated to confronting the world epidemics of nonmarital pregnancy and sexually transmitted disease, with incisive health care data. The institute stresses abstinence until marriage as the only guaranteed method of preventing nonmarital pregnancy and sexually transmitted disease. It publishes *STDs: The Facts Brochure* and the newsletter *Sexual Health Update.*

National AIDS Fund
1400 I St. NW, Suite 1220, Washington, DC 20005
(202) 408-4848 • fax: (202) 408-1818
e-mail: info@aidsfund.org • website: www.aidsfund.org

The fund seeks to eliminate AIDS as a major health and social problem. Its members work in partnership with the public and private sectors to provide care and to prevent new infections by means of advocacy, grants, research, and education. The fund publishes the monthly newsletter *News from the National AIDS Fund.*

National Institute of Allergy and Infectious Diseases (NIAID)
Office of Communications
Building 31, Room 7A-5031 Center Dr., MSC 2520, Bethesda, MD 20892-2520
e-mail: ocpostoffice@flash.niaid.nih.gov • website: www.niaid.nih.gov

NIAID is the program of the National Institutes of Health that deals with AIDS and sexually transmitted diseases. The institute conducts and supports research on diagnostic tests, treatments, and vaccines, and carries out epidemiological studies. It publishes a monthly newsletter, information on its research activities, and many informational publications, including *Sexually Transmitted Diseases: An Introduction* and *HIV and Adolescents.*

Planned Parenthood Federation of America
810 Seventh Ave., New York, NY 10019
(212) 541-7800 • fax: (212) 245-1845
e-mail: communications@ppfa.org • website: www.plannedparenthood.org

Planned Parenthood believes that all individuals should have access to comprehensive sexuality education in order to make decisions about their own fertility. It publishes information on protecting against STDs and AIDS.

Index

Index